OFF-GRID HOMESTEADING FOR BEGINNERS

A STEP-BY-STEP GUIDE TO CREATING A SELF-SUFFICIENT, ECO-FRIENDLY HOME FOR FINANCIAL FREEDOM

WELLNESS WISDOM WORKS

WELLNESS WISDOM WORKS

TABLE OF CONTENTS

INTRODUCTION

In a world where the relentless pace of urban life often leaves us feeling disconnected from our roots, the vision of a serene, self-sufficient homestead is a beacon of hope and tranquility. This vision, born out of yearning for simplicity and a deeper connection with the earth, has guided my journey from a conventional, urban existence to a more sustainable lifestyle, one lived in harmony with nature instead of in opposition to it.

This book is not just a collection of ideas but a practical tool to help you navigate the complexities of sustainable living practices, renewable energy sources, and the principles of financial freedom. It springs from a sincere desire to empower, educate, and inspire those transitioning to an off-grid lifestyle. It provides a practical roadmap, leading you from selecting your piece of earth to achieving energy independence and food security. We understand that making a significant lifestyle change can be exciting and daunting. However, with the proper knowledge and tools, you can overcome these challenges and forge your path to self-sufficiency. This guide is here to provide you with those tools and knowledge.

The transformative potential of off-grid homesteading is immense, extending far beyond the physical realm. It promotes a profound shift in mindset, health, and overall well-being. As you embark on this journey, you will gain self-reliance and experience a deep peace from reconnecting with nature. Most importantly, you will find fulfillment in living in alignment with your values and a sense of purpose often elusive in the modern world.

However, it's also essential to approach this journey with open eyes and acknowledge the challenges ahead. These challenges may include adapting to a new lifestyle, learning new skills, and managing resources effectively. But remember, the rewards are equally significant. You will experience freedom, fulfillment, and a deeper connection with nature. This book is here to equip you with the knowledge and tools you need to overcome these hurdles, fostering a sense of optimism and confidence every step of the way. But remember, you are not alone in this journey. The community of aspiring homesteaders is here to support and guide you. Together, we can make this transition to off-grid homesteading a fulfilling and rewarding experience.

As we stand at the threshold of this adventure, I urge you to approach this book with an open heart and a willingness to learn. The path to off-grid homesteading is as rewarding as the destination itself, and every small step you take brings you closer to realizing your dream lifestyle. Please actively engage with the content, ask questions, and share your experiences. Together, we can make this journey to off-grid homesteading a fulfilling and rewarding experience, and I'd like to share a reflection:

The actual value of a life well-lived is not measured by the possessions we acquire but by the harmony we create with the world around us.

As you turn the page and begin your journey, remember that the most profound transformations often bring us closer to our authentic selves and the natural world. I look forward to encouraging you on your transformative journey into off-grid homesteading.

1

LAND ASSESSMENT AND LEGAL CONSIDERATIONS

Crafting a life in harmony with nature's rhythms has a powerful allure. Yet underneath this idyllic vision lies a complex mosaic of legalities and practicalities, things you need to consider before laying the foundation of your sustainable community. The intricacies of zoning laws and land assessment might not be as captivating as planting heirloom seeds or capturing the sun's energy. Still, they are undeniably critical to establishing a homestead that can thrive. Before we delve into tips to start your homestead, let's take a second to review these big-picture land considerations that will ensure your property's legality, sustainability, and future success. Understanding these laws and restrictions empowers you to make informed decisions. It puts you in control of shaping your homestead according to your vision, instilling confidence in your journey.

RESEARCH LOCAL ZONING LAWS

Before laying the first stone or planting the first tree, a homesteader must become acquainted with the local, state, and federal regulations that govern their land. This knowledge serves as a shield and compass, guiding you through the legal landscape and safeguarding you against potential pitfalls.

Zoning laws, the backbone of land use in the United States, dictate activities on a given parcel of land. These laws impact everything from the type of structures you can build to the animals you can raise. For instance, agricultural zoning typically allows for keeping livestock, crop production, and the construction of barns and other agricultural structures. Laws may restrict these activities or require special permits under residential zoning laws.

The first crucial step for aspiring homesteaders is visiting their local zoning office or their municipality's website. Here, you'll find maps and documents outlining the zoning classifications for your area. These classifications can range from residential to agricultural, commercial, or industrial. Understanding these classifications is paramount as they directly impact your homesteading plans. Suppose you envision a lush vegetable garden and raising chickens, but your land is zoned strictly for residential use. In that case, you may need to apply for a variance or special permit to avoid costly mistakes and legal battles.

NAVIGATING PROPERTY RESTRICTIONS

Beyond zoning laws, property restrictions such as easements or covenants, conditions, and restrictions (CC&Rs) can influence your homesteading activities. An easement might grant a neighbor or utility company the right to use a portion of your property, potentially limiting where you can build structures or dig wells. CC&Rs, often set by homeowners' associations (HOAs), can impose additional rules, from the types of animals allowed to the color of your exterior paint.

If you own your property, your deed and associated documents should outline existing easements, covenants, and restrictions. If you're still searching for land, ensure you know the CC&Rs or easements attached to any properties you're considering. Understanding these limitations early on can spare you costly mistakes and legal battles. If there's a utility easement running through your proposed vegetable garden site, knowing that in advance will let you adjust your plans, ensuring both legal compliance and the uninterrupted growth of your garden.

Legal Considerations for Building

Permits and building codes apply whenever you erect structures on your homestead, whether a cozy cabin or a greenhouse. These regulations ensure that buildings meet safety standards, minimize the risk of structural failures, and ensure the well-being of occupants.

Before breaking ground, contacting your local building department to inquire about the necessary permits is crucial. This process might involve submitting detailed plans for review, undergoing inspections, and paying associated fees. While it might seem like a hurdle, this step is vital for ensuring your structures are safe, legal, and insurable. Adhering to building codes and obtaining the proper permits is a non-negotiable part of establishing a sustainable and legal homestead.

Advocating for Your Rights

Zoning laws may not set the current restrictions on a property. If these regulations clash with your vision, seeking a variance or amendment to zoning laws can be a pathway to legally realizing your homesteading dreams. While it may seem daunting, it's important to remember that change is possible. With the right approach and a well-reasoned argument, you can advocate for your rights and shape the zoning laws to align with your homesteading vision. This process is possible and within your reach, giving you hope and encouragement to pursue your dreams and instilling a sense of optimism and determination in your homesteading journey.

This process usually involves presenting your case to a zoning board or local council. Highlighting how your plans align with broader community values or how they might benefit the area can strengthen your case. Demonstrate how your homestead will embrace sustainability, bolster local food security, or preserve green space to show it will help the whole neighborhood. Gather signatures, testimonials, or other indications that you have the community's support, if possible.

In this legal landscape, knowledge is power, and preparation is critical. Arm yourself thoroughly with knowledge of the existing zoning and property laws that apply to your land. This understanding allows you to make informed decisions, adapt your plans as necessary, and advocate effectively for your homesteading vision. Once you have this knowledge base, develop a well-reasoned argument for your proposal.

ASSESSING LAND FOR WATER RESOURCES

Water is the lifeblood of any homestead. It dictates the viability of agricultural endeavors and is just as critical for your and your family's daily sustenance. Establishing an off-grid homestead requires meticulously evaluating available water sources. You also need to consider the legality of its use, the purity of its composition, and its capacity to sustain both human life and agriculture. The importance of water in homesteading cannot be overstated; it is a top priority that demands your immediate attention, highlighting the urgency and priority of this aspect in your homesteading journey.

Identifying Water Sources

The search for water on your land is a critical task. Start by surveying the land and identifying any natural bodies of water, such as streams, lakes, or springs. Look for signs of water, such as lush vegetation or damp soil. These features enhance the landscape's beauty and serve as potential cornerstones of a homestead's water supply. However, the mere presence of water doesn't guarantee its accessibility or legal availability. Local and state laws weave a complex tapestry of water rights, dictating how to utilize these natural resources. Understanding these laws is essential to ensure a sustainable and legal water supply for your homestead.

For lands lacking natural water features, wells present a feasible alternative by tapping into underground aquifers. While financially and technically demanding, drilling a well offers a degree of autonomy in water supply management. However, it's crucial to remember that well-drilling projects are subject to legal scrutiny and regulatory compliance. Understanding what permits you need and the environmental guidelines and standards you must adhere to during drilling and when using the water you access is essential. This knowledge will help you plan your well-drilling project effectively and ensure that your homestead's water supply is sustainable and legal.

Water Quality Testing

Once you identify a potential water source, you must thoroughly test its suitability for consumption and agriculture. Testing for pH levels, contaminants like heavy metals or pesticides, and microbial activity gives insights into the water's quality and purification needs. Local extension offices or environmental agencies supply testing kits that can provide a snapshot of the water's health and usability.

Filtration and purification systems are essential when water quality falls below safe consumption thresholds. These systems range from manual processes like boiling to complex reverse osmosis installations. Each purification method has its considerations, from financial cost to maintenance demands. We'll dig deeper into choosing and implementing water purification systems in Chapter 8. However, when selecting a homestead site, understand your potential water sources and what modifications they may require to ensure a safe and reliable water supply.

Rainwater Harvesting Potential

In addition to natural water sources and wells, rainwater harvesting is a sustainable supplement to a homestead's water strategy. This practice, rooted in collecting and storing rainwater, hinges on analyzing local rainfall patterns and the land's topography. Factors such as the average annual rainfall, the distribution of precipitation throughout the year, and the surface area available for collection are critical in determining the feasibility and scale of a rainwater harvesting system.

A successful rainwater harvesting setup includes:

- Catchment surfaces, often the roofs of buildings
- Storage tanks for the collected water
- Filtration systems render the water suitable for use

Integrating a rainwater reclamation system diversifies the homestead's water sources and enhances the property's sustainability by capturing a resource that would otherwise escape as runoff.

Irrigation Needs and Solutions

Adequate water supply extends into agriculture and livestock care, which dictates the crops and animals the land supports. A strategic approach to irrigation begins with understanding the water demand inherent to different agricultural practices, from the intensive requirements of vegetable gardens to the more moderate needs of orchards.

Several sustainable irrigation options are mindful of water conservation and efficiency. Drip irrigation systems deliver water directly to the roots of plants, reducing waste and minimizing evaporation. Techniques such as mulching further enhance water retention in the soil, complementing irrigation efforts with natural moisture preservation methods.

For livestock, developing water distribution systems that ensure constant access to clean water is paramount. Consider installing automatic watering devices that refill consistently, safeguarding the animals' health and easing the manual labor involved in their care.

In orchestrating these water resources and systems, a homestead finds harmony between its inhabitants' needs and the land's offerings. The careful assessment and management of water, from its source to its application, anchors the homestead in principles of sustainability, resourcefulness, and respect for the natural world.

SOIL TESTING FOR AGRICULTURE

Soil, a dynamic and living entity, plays a pivotal role in the success of agricultural endeavors. It's not merely the medium in which plants grow but a complex ecosystem vital to their nutrition and overall health. Different soil types, from sandy to clay, each hold unique characteristics that influence water retention, nutrient availability, and aeration. Understanding these properties is the first step toward growing healthy, productive gardens and crops.

Conducting soil tests is the best way to gauge its health and suitability for specific crops. These tests offer valuable insights into pH levels, nutrient content, and the presence of potential contaminants. A balanced pH is crucial for plants to optimize nutrient uptake, while the nutrient profile tells you what supplements you'll need to provide. Additionally, early detection of contaminants can help avert potential health hazards and inform necessary cleanup measures.

The excellent news is soil testing is often a straightforward process. Many local cooperative extension services offer testing services or kits, providing detailed instructions for sample collection. Typically, this involves gathering soil from several locations and depths within your plot to ensure a representative sample. Once collected and sent to a lab, the wait time for results averages a few weeks. These tests not only shed light on the current state of your soil but serve as a guide for amendments and improvements.

To enhance soil fertility naturally, consider these organic methods:

- Composting: By converting kitchen scraps and yard waste into compost, you enrich the soil with diverse nutrients and beneficial microorganisms. This practice bolsters plant health and contributes to a closed-loop system, reducing waste and reliance on external inputs.
- Cover cropping: Growing cover crops like clover or rye in the off-season protects the soil from erosion, suppresses weeds, and fixes nitrogen, a vital nutrient for plant growth. When tilled back into the soil, cover crops decompose, improving soil structure and fertility.

- Crop rotation: Rotating crops in a planned sequence can break pest and disease cycles, reduce soil erosion, and enhance soil structure and fertility. Different crops have varying nutrient needs and contributions, making rotation a strategy that sustains soil health over time.

A proactive approach is vital to overcome common soil challenges. To address issues like erosion, compaction, and poor drainage, you can apply the following solutions:

- Erosion control: Implementing barriers such as hedgerows or planting cover crops can significantly reduce soil loss due to wind or water. Terracing sloped land also minimizes runoff, preserving topsoil.
- Alleviating compaction: Regular aeration of the soil, avoiding heavy machinery, and incorporating organic matter can relieve compaction, which improves root penetration, water infiltration, and aeration, fostering a healthier root environment.
- Improving drainage: For areas prone to waterlogging, creating raised beds or installing drainage systems like French drains can enhance soil drainage, preventing root rot and other moisture-related issues.

Through these practices, homesteaders can nurture their soil, turning potential challenges into opportunities for growth and sustainability.

SOLAR AND WIND POTENTIAL ANALYSIS

Harnessing the power of the elements to create a renewable energy source is both practical and environmentally conscious. Solar and wind energies are abundant and freely available, offering a path to energy independence. However, they also require careful consideration and planning to implement. Assessing a property's renewable energy potential before starting your homestead construction can help you choose suitable sources and benefit most from them.

Evaluating Solar Exposure

Optimal sunlight exposure is critical to tapping into solar energy effectively. Begin by understanding the sun's path across your property throughout the year, considering any potential obstructions like tall trees or buildings that might cast shadows on solar panel installations. Tools like solar pathfinders or apps that simulate solar positions can be invaluable in this assessment. For homes, incorporating passive solar design—strategically placing windows, selecting materials with thermal mass properties, and utilizing overhangs for summer shade—can significantly reduce heating and cooling needs.

Wind Energy Feasibility

Wind turbines convert the wind's kinetic energy into electrical power, an excellent complement to solar energy. Wind speed assessment can tell you if your land is suitable for a wind turbine. Ideally, an average wind speed of at least 10 miles per hour is required to use this energy source. Anemometers that measure wind speed can collect data over time to ensure accuracy. It is important to research local regulations before planning if you're considering an on-site wind turbine. Some areas restrict the height of structures, which could limit turbine effectiveness.

Hybrid Systems for Reliability

While both solar and wind energy have their strengths, they also have limitations related to weather conditions and time of day. A hybrid system that combines solar panels and wind turbines can offer excellent reliability and a more consistent energy supply. Solar panels can capture sunlight during sunny but calm days, while windy or overcast days can increase wind turbines' output. Integrating these systems requires a well-designed setup with a compatible inverter and battery storage to manage the varying inputs from both energy sources.

Cost-Benefit Analysis

Investing in renewable energy systems can involve substantial upfront costs. On the other hand, they often also mean significant long-term savings and benefits. Conducting a cost-benefit analysis starts by estimating the total costs to purchase, install, and maintain the equipment. Compare these costs against the projected savings on utility bills, possible tax incentives, and rebates. Tools like solar calculators or consultations with renewable energy professionals can provide personalized estimates, helping to make informed decisions. Also, the intangible benefits, such as the environmental impact of reducing fossil fuel consumption and the peace of mind with energy independence, should be considered.

Adopting renewable energy is more than a financial decision; it's a commitment to a sustainable and self-sufficient lifestyle. While the initial steps require careful planning and analysis, the long-term rewards of harnessing the power of the sun and wind are immeasurable, providing a foundation for a resilient and eco-friendly homestead.

PRIVACY VS. ACCESSIBILITY: FINDING YOUR BALANCE

The allure of off-grid homesteading often includes solitude and life removed from the hustle of urban centers. Complete isolation isn't practical for everyone, though. When planning your homestead's location, it's essential to think about your daily life needs and what you'll do in an emergency. Striking a balance between the tranquility of seclusion and the accessibility of necessary services is a nuanced exercise that requires careful deliberation.

Trade-offs between Seclusion and Access

Living off the grid doesn't inherently mean forsaking all the conveniences of modern life. Proximity to local markets, healthcare facilities, and community resources plays a significant role in the sustainability of a homestead lifestyle. On one hand, a more remote location might offer greater privacy and a deeper connection with nature, fulfilling a profound desire for many aspiring homesteaders. Conversely, being too far removed from essential services makes daily errands more time-consuming and more challenging to prepare for emergencies.

When evaluating potential properties, consider what modern conveniences you need or value and which you are willing to compromise for privacy. For some, being within a 30-minute drive of a healthcare facility is non-negotiable. In contrast, others might prioritize easy access to a community of like-minded individuals over proximity to commercial services.

Road Access and Maintenance

The practicality of accessing your homestead, particularly in adverse weather conditions, is critical. First of all, the legal right-of-way must be clear. Ensure your property has deeded access, preventing disputes over driveways or access roads with neighbors. Also, make sure you know who is responsible for maintaining the condition of these roads. A private, unmaintained road might offer more seclusion but also comes with the responsibility and cost of upkeep, including snow removal in colder climates or grading and graveling to prevent erosion.

Some questions to ponder include:

- Is the access road to the property public or private?
- If it is private, who is responsible for its maintenance?
- What is the condition of the road, and how does it fare in different seasons?

These considerations affect your day-to-day life, property value, and emergency access.

Proximity to Emergency Services

The location of your homestead relative to emergency services such as fire departments, hospitals, and police stations can significantly impact response times in critical situations. Fully embracing the off-grid lifestyle means preparing for and mitigating many risks independently, but some emergencies require professional intervention, even if you're predominantly self-sufficient.

To assess the implications of your land's location on emergency services:

- Map out the distance and driving time to the nearest hospital, fire station, and police station.
- Consider the availability of ambulance and roadside assistance services in your area.
- For properties in areas prone to natural disasters like wildfires or flooding, understand local emergency response strategies and how your property fits into them.

Engaging with local emergency services and understanding their capabilities and limitations ensures you are better prepared for any situation.

Community Connections

While the desire for privacy might drive the decision to live off-grid, human connections remain vital to well-being. Engaging with local communities and networks can offer support, enrich your homestead life, and provide a sense of belonging. This engagement can take many forms, from participating in local farmers' markets and community events to joining or initiating cooperative projects focused on sustainability.

Building these connections while maintaining the level of privacy you desire is possible through the following:

- Volunteering for community projects or local environmental initiatives.
- Consider hosting workshops or open days on your homestead to share knowledge and skills related to sustainable living, inviting the community into your world on your terms.
- Online platforms and social media, which connect with local and global communities interested in homesteading, sustainability, and self-sufficiency, are valuable resources.

These efforts bridge the gap between seclusion and community engagement. Embedding your homestead within a mutual support network and shared values strengthens its resilience.

In navigating the balance between privacy and accessibility, remember that each decision shapes the fabric of your homesteading experience. The location of your homestead influences not just your daily routines and practicalities but also your interactions with other people and the natural environment. The key lies in identifying what matters most to you and making informed choices that reflect your priorities and aspirations for off-grid living.

2

FINANCIAL FOUNDATIONS FOR OFF-GRID SUCCESS

Envision yourself in a thriving garden, a testament to your perseverance and commitment, with the sun setting behind your solar-powered home. This idyllic scene, while alluring, is a far cry from the starting point. The path to this point commences with a robust financial plan. Just as a solid foundation is essential for a well-constructed home, sound financial planning is the cornerstone of a successful homestead. Let's explore the initial financial considerations pivotal in turning the dream of off-grid living into a reality and the accompanying sense of achievement and satisfaction.

INITIAL COSTS BREAKDOWN

The precise costs for setting up an off-grid homestead can vary significantly, and numerous factors influence these expenditures. These factors encompass whether you're starting from scratch or converting an existing dwelling, the scale and extent of your homesteading plans, and which aspects of the project you feel confident handling yourself. While the specific amounts may differ, there are some fundamental categories of expenses that every new homesteader should anticipate before planting the first seed or hammering the first nail. These categories include:

- Land purchase: Land is the cornerstone of your homesteading endeavor. Prices vary widely based on location, size, and available resources (such as water and fertile soil).
- Construction: Construction costs can be substantial, whether building a new structure or renovating an existing one. These costs cover your home, any additional buildings, and essential infrastructure such as roads.
- Solar/wind setup: Investing in renewable energy systems upfront can lead to long-term savings, but it requires a substantial initial outlay. Funding includes the cost of energy storage systems and renewable energy infrastructure.
- Starting livestock and gardens: The costs include purchasing seedlings, seeds, soil amendments, and any initial livestock, along with their feed and shelter needs.

Along with planning for the known costs, it's wise to budget extra funds for unexpected expenses that come up along the way. Unforeseen costs and challenges are a given in any substantial project. Setting aside a contingency fund—typically 10-20% of your projected budget—can provide a safety net for unexpected costs, from a sudden rise in material prices to emergency repairs. A contingency fund is a reserve of money you can tap into when unexpected expenses arise. It's like an insurance policy for your budget, ensuring you're prepared for the unexpected.

Prioritizing Investments

Even with adequate planning, you may find yourself in a position where your current budget doesn't entirely cover all of your anticipated expenses upfront. In these situations, prioritizing becomes critical. A helpful strategy is to focus on investments that offer immediate utility or long-term savings. For example, securing a reliable water source and establishing your energy system are critical early steps for establishing a viable homestead. Similarly, investing in quality tools and equipment that will stand the test of time can prevent more costly replacements. This approach ensures your immediate needs are met and paves the way for long-term financial sustainability. It's a path to security and stability, providing you with the confidence that you're on the right track.

SEEKING FINANCIAL ASSISTANCE

The financial demands of starting a homestead can be overwhelming, but there are numerous avenues of financial assistance to help you overcome this hurdle. These options encompass:

- Loans: These commonly take the form of traditional mortgages, land, or construction loans. For those pursuing agriculture, there are also specific loans catering to the needs of small farmers, such as the USDA Farm Service Agency (FSA) loans, which offer low interest rates and flexible terms.
- Grants: Government and private grants can offer non-repayable funds for specific projects, especially those focused on sustainability, conservation, or renewable energy.

- Cost-sharing programs: Programs that share the cost of certain agricultural or conservation practices can significantly reduce your financial burden.
- Community support: Crowdfunding or community-supported agriculture (CSA) models can also provide initial funding, leveraging the support of your future customers or community. This helps financially and fosters a sense of community and support. Knowing you're not alone in this endeavor is a way to feel connected and encouraged in your homesteading journey.

Conducting thorough research on the eligibility requirements is crucial when considering these options. Local agricultural extensions or renewable energy organizations can be invaluable resources, offering tailored guidance for your area and situation. Here's more advice on how to make the most of these financial assistance options.

Grants and Financial Aid for Homesteaders

The availability of grants and financial aid opens doors to opportunities that budget restraints might otherwise close. These resources require diligence, strategy, and a deep understanding of the available support landscape. Each region and situation will present its options, but here is a general overview of obtaining financial aid.

Researching Available Grants

Grants are awarded for particular purposes. Because of this, you are finding a grant and need to start clearly understanding your homesteading goals. Are you focusing on sustainable agriculture, renewable energy integration, or community development? Identifying your key objectives can help determine the grants you will most likely successfully obtain.

Once you know your goals, the next phase involves meticulous research. Numerous databases and websites cater to agriculture, sustainability, and rural project grants. The key to this exploration is finding opportunities and discerning what aligns most closely with your homesteading vision and values.

Many homesteaders find it most productive to start with government agricultural sites, which are often rich sources of grant listings. You can explore non-profit organizations dedicated to sustainability and rural development or consider academic institutions and cooperative extension offices. Use keywords related to your project, such as 'sustainable agriculture grants' or 'rural development grants,' to narrow your search results when searching for grants.

Eligibility and Application Process

Each grant has eligibility criteria, ranging from the project's scope to your homestead's location. Understanding these requirements keeps you from expending energy on applications that don't fit. Once you've identified a grant as a potential match, pay close attention to the details during the application process. It's also essential to clearly articulate your project's goals, expected outcomes, and benefits. Tips for a successful application include:

- Thoroughly read application guidelines and adhere to them strictly.
- Provide clear, concise descriptions of your project backed by data where applicable.
- Highlight the sustainability and community benefits of your project to stand out.

Leveraging Local and State Resources

Often, the support you need is closer than you think. The narrower geographic eligibility of local and state resources can make these funds more attainable. Look for extension services that offer grant information and workshops on writing successful proposals. Agricultural programs at state levels may have funds designated for supporting small farms and homesteads in their transition to sustainable practices.

Attending grant writing workshops and seminars offered through agricultural programs can be an excellent way to discover these opportunities and be more successful in your applications. Don't forget the power of a personal connection, either. Talking with a local extension agent can give you insights into opportunities precisely matched to your unique needs or situation. Networking with other homesteaders or small farmers at local markets or community events allows you to learn from their experiences. It can be another excellent way to learn about financial aid opportunities.

Crowdfunding and Community Support

Income Generation Strategies

- Craft a compelling story that resonates with potential supporters, highlighting the impact of their contribution.
- Potential Risks and Challenges
- The Financial Planning Process for Off-Grid Homesteading

This is an excellent opportunity to remind you that securing crowdfunding or CSA support is more than a means to an end. It invites others to join in your commitment to sustainable living. With each crowdfunding campaign launched or CSA share sold, you weave a more substantial, resilient fabric for your homestead while contributing to the broader tapestry of sustainable, off-grid living.

LONG-TERM FINANCIAL PLANNING

In the analogy of off-grid homesteading as a tapestry, each thread represents a different aspect of sustainable living. Long-term financial planning is the loom that holds everything together. It ensures the fabric of your homestead has a tight weave that remains strong and resilient through the seasons. This section will guide you through projecting future expenses, building a robust savings plan, investing wisely in self-sufficiency, and understanding the nuances of insurance coverage.

Projecting Future Expenses

Anticipating the ongoing financial demands of your homestead requires understanding the broader economic landscape, from the peaks of annual property taxes to the valleys of day-to-day utility costs. Key areas to consider include:

- Maintenance costs: Buildings, machinery, and systems all require regular upkeep. Setting aside funds for the maintenance of your home, outbuildings, renewable energy installations, and water systems ensures they continue to serve you effectively.
- Energy and water: Even when you live off-grid, there are costs associated with power and water. Solar system batteries have a lifespan and will need replacing. Similarly, water purification filters and parts for water

pumps will also wear out with time and require periodic replacement.
- Livestock care: Animals bring joy and sustenance but require feed, medical care, and possibly emergency veterinary services. Estimating these costs upfront helps you to plan for their well-being.
- Agricultural inputs: Seeds, seedlings, soil amendments, and natural pest control solutions are recurring expenses necessary to keep your garden and crops thriving.

Building a Savings Plan

A savings plan is a financial safety net that empowers you to embrace new opportunities without derailing your homesteading dreams. It's wise to dedicate certain portions of your savings for specific purposes. These often include:

- Emergency funds: Aim to maintain a reserve that covers six months to a year of living expenses, protecting you against unexpected events that could compromise your homestead's stability.
- Savings for future expansions and improvements: Dedicate a portion of your savings to your homestead's future growth. Whether expanding your garden, adding more solar panels, or building a greenhouse, having funds allocated for these projects keeps your homestead vibrant, vibrant, and evolving.
- Retirement savings: Off-grid living doesn't exempt you from planning for retirement. Consider retirement accounts that align with your self-employed or small business status, ensuring your financial independence continues into your later years.

Investing in Self-Sufficiency

Investments in self-sufficiency are strategic moves that reduce operational costs over time, enhancing your homestead's financial resilience. When making these investments, focus on:

- Renewable energy systems: Solar panels and wind turbines may have upfront costs, but they dramatically decrease your long-term energy expenses. Calculate the break-even point to understand how these systems pay for themselves through savings.
- Water systems: A reliable, self-sustaining water system, including wells, rainwater catchment, and purification setups, mitigates the need for municipal water, reducing monthly costs and increasing your autonomy.
- Efficient buildings and insulation: Investing in well-insulated homes and outbuildings minimizes energy loss, reducing the need for heating and cooling. This upfront investment pays dividends in comfort and savings for years to come.

Insurance Considerations

Insuring an off-grid homestead can be complex, yet it's a critical component of your financial planning. Adequate insurance coverage safeguards your investment by protecting against catastrophic losses. Key areas include:

- Property insurance: Ensure your policy covers your property's structures, including homes, outbuildings, and installations like solar arrays or wind turbines.
- Crop and livestock insurance: Specialized insurance policies can cover livestock loss or crop failure due to extreme

weather conditions. These protections can be pivotal in preserving one's financial health through adversity.

- Liability insurance: If you open your homestead to the public through tours, workshops, or as a bed and breakfast, liability insurance protects you against claims for injury and damage to your property.

Insurance may seem like an unnecessary expense when things are going smoothly, but it is a critical thread in your homestead's financial fabric to enhance the resilience of the whole. By proactively protecting your investment, you ensure your homestead thrives for years.

ALTERNATIVE INCOME SOURCES ON YOUR HOMESTEAD

The magic of a homestead lies not just in its ability to sustain a family's needs but also in its potential to become a source of income, transforming the homestead from a place of personal fulfillment into a beacon of economic independence. With strategic planning and creativity, you can generate multiple revenue streams from your land to support the lifestyle you cherish.

Diversifying Income Streams

A diverse income portfolio ensures stability and growth. Consider these avenues:

- Farmers' markets: Local markets are the ideal place to sell surplus produce, homemade preserves, artisanal bread, or other food you grow or make. They provide income and connect you with the community. When you establish a consistent selling pattern at specific markets, you can build a loyal customer base over time and, through that, a consistent income stream.

- Online sales: Digital marketplaces offer boundless opportunities, extending your reach beyond your local area. Popular items to sell include seeds from your heirloom plants, handmade crafts, or digital guides on sustainable living. A solid online presence and understanding of digital marketing strategies are essential to thriving in this space.
- Agritourism: Inviting guests to experience the beauty and tranquility of your homestead can be a significant income source. From day visits where families learn about sustainable farming to weekend retreats that offer a deeper immersion into off-grid living, agritourism caters to the growing desire for meaningful, nature-connected experiences. Liability insurance and excellent hospitality skills are prerequisites for this venture.
- Bed and Breakfast: Transforming part of your homestead into a bed and breakfast caters to those seeking a rustic getaway. Success in this venture often hinges on creating a cozy, welcoming environment and providing guests with a unique, memorable experience.
- Workshops: Sharing your skills and knowledge through workshops or courses can be deeply rewarding. Whether it's organic gardening, woodworking, or natural building techniques, these educational offerings can attract individuals eager to learn and apply sustainable living practices.

- Product sales: Your homestead's unique products, natural skincare items made from your herbs, or handcrafted furniture from your woodlot have a market. The trick lies in identifying your niche, ensuring product quality, and effectively reaching your target audience.

Renewable Energy Incentives

The shift towards renewable energy is not just an ecological decision but a financially astute one. Various government programs offer incentives for homesteads that produce excess renewable energy, allowing them to sell back to the grid. These incentives include:

- Feed-in Tariffs (FITs): These policies guarantee a fixed, premium rate for renewable energy fed back into the grid over a specified period. Navigating these requires understanding local energy policies and negotiating contracts with utility providers.
- Renewable Energy Certificates (RECs): By generating renewable energy, your homestead earns RECs, which can be sold to businesses looking to offset their carbon footprint. This system provides additional income and contributes to the broader goal of reducing global carbon emissions.

Financial Sustainability

Creating a sustainable financial model for your homestead intertwines the threads of income generation with the principles of sustainable living. Choosing which income-generating activities are suitable for you can be challenging. The best metric for this is to start from your values, lifestyle, and homesteading goals.

Aligning your financial activities with these important intangibles fosters a greater sense of fulfillment and purpose, making them more long-term sustainable.

While your values and lifestyle are a great place to start, it's also essential to consider the market's needs and trends. Stay flexible and be ready to pivot your offerings to meet shifting demands, ensuring your homestead remains relevant and financially viable.

Finally, consider how you use the income earned from your homestead. Reinvest some of it into infrastructure improvements, like expanding renewable energy capacity or enhancing agritourism facilities. This kind of reinvestment fuels growth and increases the value of your offerings.

BUDGETING FOR HOMESTEAD IMPROVEMENTS

Whether expanding your living space, enhancing your garden's productivity, or upgrading to more efficient energy systems, each improvement you make to your homestead is a step toward realizing its full potential. These growth cycles mirror the natural rhythms that dictate rural life. Successfully navigating these phases starts with strategic planning and mindful budgeting, ensuring that each project meets your current needs and contributes to your long-term vision.

Planning for Growth and Improvements

A tactical approach to planning for homestead expansions and enhancements begins with setting clear objectives. What are your goals for the coming year, and what projects will help you achieve those goals? Once you've identified these targets, outline a timeline and budget for each, including phases of research, sourcing materials, and actual construction or installation, with each phase assigned a specific timeframe and cost estimate that includes both material costs and labor.

Cost-effective Building and Renovation

The ethos of homesteading often leans towards doing more with less. For building and renovation projects, this could mean:

- DIY projects: Tackling projects yourself can significantly reduce labor costs. Online tutorials, community workshops, and local homesteading groups can be excellent resources for learning new skills.
- Reclaimed materials: Utilizing reclaimed or recycled materials lowers expenses and aligns with the sustainability principles that many homesteaders value. Salvage yards, online marketplaces, and community networks can be treasure troves of affordable, repurposed building materials.
- Community resource sharing: Borrowing tools or equipment from neighbors or local co-ops reduces the need for individual purchases. In return, you can offer your skills or resources, fostering community and mutual support.

Upgrading for Efficiency

Investing in upgrades that enhance efficiency and sustainability pays dividends over time, reducing operational costs and minimizing environmental impact. Include the following:

- Insulation: Improving your home's insulation reduces the need for heating and cooling. Materials like spray foam, wool, or recycled denim are effective and eco-friendly.

- Water systems: Upgrading to more efficient water systems, such as drip irrigation for gardens or low-flow fixtures for homes, conserves water and lowers utility bills.
- Renewable energy sources: Adding or expanding solar panels, wind turbines, or hydroelectric systems increases energy independence and reduces reliance on fossil fuels.

Consider the long-term savings alongside the initial investment when budgeting for these upgrades. Grants or incentives are often available for projects that improve energy efficiency or sustainability, further offsetting costs.

Tracking Expenses and ROI

For homesteaders, every dollar spent on their land and lifestyle is significant. Thus, it is crucial to carefully track expenses and assess the return on investment (ROI) for any improvements made to the homestead. Doing so provides essential insights for current and future decisions by identifying the most beneficial investments. Tracking your expenses is the first step in this process. Keep detailed records of all expenses related to homestead improvements, from the cost of materials to any hired labor. Digital tools and apps can simplify this, allowing for easy categorization and analysis of your spending.

When you embark on a new project, you can use those tracked expenses to calculate your projected ROI accurately. Once the project is complete and operational, you can determine its actual return on investment by comparing the total cost against the value it adds to your homestead. For energy upgrades, calculate the savings on utility bills over time. Consider the increased functionality and potential property value appreciation for expansions or renovations and any direct cost reduction or income it yields.

Finally, ensure you regularly review your expenses and completed project outcomes. This reflection can reveal insights into spending patterns, cost-saving opportunities, and your homestead's financial health.

By adopting a systematic budgeting approach, you ensure that each project meets your immediate needs and contributes to the sustainability and growth of your homestead over time. Whether through DIY initiatives, strategic upgrades, or the prudent management of finances, each step reflects your commitment to a lifestyle that values self-reliance, environmental stewardship, and the continual pursuit of improvement.

3

SUSTAINABLE HOMESTEAD DESIGN

Imagine you're planting a tree. You wouldn't just toss it into the ground and hope for the best. You'd carefully consider its needs for sunlight, water, and soil. Like planting that tree, designing a sustainable homestead requires intention and understanding of the natural environment. It's about creating a space that supports your lifestyle and thrives alongside the local ecosystem. This chapter explores the foundational principles of permaculture as a blueprint for achieving such harmony, blending ancient wisdom with modern sustainability practices to cultivate a thriving homestead.

PRINCIPLES OF PERMACULTURE DESIGN

Permaculture is a portmanteau of 'permanent agriculture,' representing more than just a gardening technique. It's a philosophy for living in harmony with the earth by mimicking the patterns found in nature, providing a framework for creating sustainable, self-sufficient homesteads. For instance, permaculture practices could include creating a food forest, where different layers of plants mimic a natural forest ecosystem, or using companion planting to enhance the health and productivity of your garden.

Understanding permaculture ethics

At the heart of permaculture lie three core ethics: care for the earth, care for people, and fair share. When understood and embraced, these principles empower you to make every decision and action within permaculture. You are in control, from the design of your garden to how you use resources. Let's take a closer look at what each of these ethics means:

- Care for the earth: This involves practices that regenerate the environment by restoring soil health, conserving water, and fostering biodiversity.
- Care for people: This ethic is about more than just self-reliance. It's about fostering a sense of community and shared responsibility. It advocates for living conditions that are sustainable and equitable, emphasizing that we are all part of the same ecosystem and have a crucial role to play in its preservation. Your homestead is not just a place for you to live but a vital part of the larger ecosystem, and by designing it sustainably, you are contributing to the health and balance of the environment.
- Fair share: This principle recognizes consumption limits and shares excess with others. It encourages a mindset of abundance rather than scarcity. By embracing this principle, you can reduce waste, foster a sense of community, and ensure everyone's needs are met without depleting resources.

Zones and sector planning

Zones in permaculture organize the homestead based on the frequency of human use, creating an efficient layout. The typical zones in a permaculture homestead are:

- Zone 0 (The Home): The center of activity, where daily life occurs.
- Zone 1 (The Kitchen Garden): Home to herbs, salads, and frequently harvested plants.
- Zone 2 (Orchards and Small Livestock): Requires less frequent attention, suitable for fruit trees and chickens.
- Zone 3 (Main Crops): Areas for larger-scale agriculture requiring minimal daily intervention.
- Zone 4 (Woodland and Forage): Less managed area used for foraging and timber.
- Zone 5 (Wilderness): A place left untouched for observation and learning from natural ecosystems.

This arrangement ensures that the most needed resources are closest to the home, reducing effort and increasing productivity.

Maximizing natural resources

A homestead thrives when it works with, not against, its environment. There are three primary natural resources that you want to consider when designing the structures and determining the zones of your property:

- Sunlight: Position gardens and solar panels in areas that receive ample sun, using the sun's path across your land as a guide.
- Wind: Natural winds can cool homes or act as a power source with wind turbines. Wind can also be destructive,

so planting windbreaks is essential to protect delicate crops or living areas.
- Water: Design landscapes to catch and store rainwater, using swales and ponds to hydrate plants and recharge groundwater.

Design your homestead to take advantage of the abundant natural areas on your property. For example, you could plant a vegetable garden on the south side of your property where it gets the most sunlight or dig a pond in a natural depression where water already tends to collect. Additionally, consider installing solar panels on your home's roof or in an open area with ample sunlight. Use windbreaks to protect delicate crops or living areas from strong winds. These strategies will help you maximize the use of natural resources on your property and reduce your reliance on external inputs, making your homestead more self-sufficient and cost-effective.

Implementing permaculture principles

Permaculture principles are abstract concepts and practical tools that empower you to create a balanced and productive homestead. You can control the process by observing, interacting with, and getting to know your land. Note the water flow, where frost pockets form, and which areas get the most sun. This knowledge will inform every other decision, giving you the confidence and capability to create a sustainable homestead.

Once you've identified the resources available in each part of your property, you can plan construction or improvements accordingly, focusing on placing energy capture infrastructure where it will be the most productive and installing it in barrels where it will be best able to collect water.

You can also make improvements that limit resource loss, such as using heavy mulch to preserve soil moisture. Additionally, implement systems that recycle waste into your homestead, like composting kitchen scraps for garden fertilizer or using greywater systems for irrigation.

Another core tenet of permaculture is mimicking the natural diversity of wild spaces. Plant various crops rather than creating a monoculture, and integrate animals into your system, mimicking natural ecosystems and reducing pests and diseases while improving yields.

For those new to these concepts, start small. Choose one area of your homestead to redesign with permaculture principles in mind. It could be a water conservation effort with a rain garden or a small kitchen garden using companion planting. Document what works and what doesn't, adjusting as you learn. Over time, these tiny changes accumulate, transforming your homestead into a model of sustainable efficiency. This journey of learning and growth, filled with inspiring moments and rewarding outcomes, is yours to shape and make fulfilling.

Permaculture offers a lens through which to view not just gardening but all aspects of living on and with the land. Its principles, grounded in care for the earth and each other, provide a roadmap for creating productive homesteads in harmony with nature.

INCORPORATING RENEWABLE ENERGY SOURCES

Tapping into the power of the sun, wind, and water provides a homestead the energy it needs to function without draining resources from the land, making renewable energy a cornerstone of sustainable self-sufficiency. Like other aspects of permaculture, integrating renewable energy into your homestead begins with observation. Note the unique characteristics of your land to identify the best systems to capture the energy it offers, and reward yourself with the satisfying hum of a well-maintained system that powers your life. Once you've identified the most viable energy source for your homestead, you can start planning the installation of the necessary infrastructure, such as solar panels or wind turbines, and consider how to integrate these systems into your overall homestead design.

Choosing the right renewable energy

There are three potential sources of renewable energy on a typical homestead:

- Solar energy is ideal for locations receiving ample sunlight throughout the year. Solar panels installed on roofs or open areas are best suited for powering household appliances and lighting.
- Wind energy is effective in open, rural areas with high wind speeds. Wind turbines can complement solar systems during overcast days.
- Hydro energy: This is a viable option for homesteads near flowing water. Micro-hydro power systems require a stream or river with a significant drop for optimal energy generation and can provide a steady power supply.

Each energy source has its optimal conditions for efficiency. A detailed assessment of your land's features and household's energy consumption can pinpoint the most viable option to meet your needs.

Remember that you don't need to choose just one renewable energy source. Combining solar and wind power, potentially supplemented by hydropower, can provide a more reliable energy supply. When one source is less productive, the other can compensate to maintain a steady power flow.

DIY vs. professional installation

DIY projects offer a sense of accomplishment and potential labor savings. They are feasible for those with a good grasp of mechanical and electrical principles. However, the complexity of specific installations, like grid-tied solar systems, may require specialized knowledge and tools that make professional installation the wiser choice.

While more costly upfront, professional installation guarantees expertise, efficiency, and, often, a warranty. Professionals also have more knowledge of local regulations and what permits are required, helping to ensure your system meets all safety standards.

Reflect on your skills, the complexity of the system, and the value of your time. For many, a hybrid approach is the best way to balance cost with the quality of the installation. You can hire professionals to handle the more intricate or specialized work where you have knowledge or skill gaps, then tackle other aspects of the work yourself to save on labor costs.

WATER CONSERVATION AND MANAGEMENT SYSTEMS

Water is the lifeblood of homesteading. It nourishes the garden that feeds your family, sustains your livestock, and supports the natural ecosystems that enrich your land. Given its vital role, the stewardship of this resource through innovative conservation and management practices is necessary for the longevity and success of your homestead.

Rainwater Harvesting Setups

Harvesting rainwater reduces your dependence on conventional water sources and aligns your homestead with the rhythms of nature. The capture and use of rainwater is as ancient as agriculture, yet modern technology has refined these systems to maximize efficiency and utility.

Customize your system's setup to suit your needs. To design it, first, map out the components and determine where they will benefit most. Installing rainwater capture systems in harmony with your land's natural resource distribution will maximize water collection and minimize the risk of contamination.

Calculating Water Catchment Capacity

Carefully calculating the potential water catchment capacity helps you size your system appropriately. To determine how much water you can expect to collect:

1. Measure your roof or collection surface's catchment area (in square feet).
2. Determine the average annual rainfall (in inches) in your area.
3. Calculate the potential capacity by multiplying the catchment area by the rainfall, then multiplying by 0.623 to convert to gallons.

This formula estimates the total gallons of water your system could collect. You can use this figure to choose the right storage tank size and guide your system's overall design.

Legal Considerations and Water Rights

Many regions support and even encourage rainwater harvesting. Others may have restrictions, especially for large-scale systems or those intended for potable use.

Before you install a rainwater harvesting system, research local ordinances and codes related to water in your area. Water rights laws may be a factor in some places, so ensure your system complies with them to avoid legal complications. More extensive systems, or those connected to your home's plumbing, may require permits. You can contact your local building department for guidance on whether you need permits and the process to apply for them.

Navigating these legal waters ensures that your rainwater harvesting system respects community resources while meeting your homestead's hydration needs.

Creating Natural Water Features

Beyond their aesthetic value, natural water features are critical in water conservation and land management. They capture runoff, recharge groundwater, and create habitats for beneficial wildlife. Some types of natural water features include:

- Ponds: Serve as reservoirs for irrigation and emergency reserves. Their location should maximize natural runoff and consider overflow routes during heavy rains.
- Swales: These shallow trenches, often planted with deep-rooted perennials, follow the contour lines of your land, slowing and capturing runoff.

- Keyline Systems: A more advanced form of water management, keyline design involves strategic plowing to spread water across the land, increasing infiltration and reducing erosion.

Incorporating these features into your landscape enhances water availability and promotes biodiversity and soil health, creating a more resilient and productive homestead.

SUSTAINABLE WASTE MANAGEMENT PRACTICES

In its myriad forms, waste is an inevitable part of life, even more so on a homestead where the cycle of growth and renewal is constant. Yet, within every discarded item or byproduct lies potential—potential for reuse, transformation, and contribution to the homestead's cycle of sustainability. This section explores practical and innovative methods for managing waste, transforming what might be considered trash into valuable resources.

Composting Organic Waste

Composting is at the core of waste transformation. This process converts kitchen scraps and yard waste into nutrient-rich soil amendments, fostering a closed-loop system that enriches the land. Various composting methods cater to different needs and scales of operation:

- Traditional composting involves layering green (nitrogen-rich) and brown (carbon-rich) materials in a bin or pile and regularly turning them to aerate. This method is suited for larger volumes of waste and requires space and physical effort.

- Vermicomposting: Uses worms, typically red wigglers, to break down organic matter in a contained system. This method is efficient, odorless, and ideal for indoor or small-space homesteaders.
- Bokashi is a fermentation process that quickly breaks down kitchen waste, including meat and dairy, using specific bran inoculated with beneficial microbes. The resulting material can be directly buried in garden beds to finish decomposing.

Each of these methods not only diverts waste from landfills but also contributes to the health of your garden, reducing the need for commercial fertilizers and enhancing soil structure.

Humanure and Composting Toilets

Human waste might be taboo, but its management is a reality for off-grid homesteaders. Composting toilets address this issue while contributing to sustainability goals. These systems use aerobic decomposition to decompose human waste into compost, enhancing the soil around non-food-bearing trees or decorative plants.

A proper setup is critical for human systems. Ensure adequate ventilation and use a carbon-rich cover material, like sawdust, to promote decomposition and eliminate odors. Adhere to recommended composting times and perform regular maintenance to kill pathogens and ensure the end product is safe.

Composting toilets have a dual appeal rooted in their ecological benefits and practicality for off-grid settings. Some of their benefits include:

- Water conservation: By sidestepping the need for flushing, these units save thousands of gallons of water annually, a boon for areas where water is scarce or conservation is a priority.
- Reduced pollution: Traditional sewage systems can strain with overload, leading to potential contamination of waterways. Composting toilets eliminate this risk by processing waste on-site.
- Soil enrichment: When properly managed, the end product is nutrient-rich compost perfect for non-edible landscaping, closing the nutrient cycle in an eco-friendly manner.
- Independence: For homesteads far from municipal sewage services, composting toilets provide a self-contained solution that's easy to install and manage.

Types of Composting Toilets

From simple designs to sophisticated systems, the variety of composting toilets caters to different needs and preferences:

- Bucket systems: The most basic form involves a bucket, a seat, and cover material like sawdust or peat moss. With diligent management, it's a cost-effective option that is surprisingly odor-free.
- Self-contained units: These all-in-one systems are suited for indoor use. They integrate the composting chamber beneath the toilet seat, making them ideal for smaller families or part-time homesteads.

- Central composting systems: More elaborate setups feature a central composting unit located away from the living area, connected to one or more toilets. This design can handle higher volumes, suitable for larger families or community settings.

Each type offers a different balance of simplicity, capacity, and maintenance needs, allowing you to tailor your choice to your homestead's specific circumstances.

Day-to-day Management and Maintenance

Toilets that empty into sewage systems need minimal attention beyond occasional cleaning, but a composting toilet needs more consistent maintenance. Their successful use starts with an understanding of the composting process and requires occasional management, including:

- Regularly adding cover material, such as sawdust, peat moss, or coconut coir, keeps odors at bay and aids in the aerobic breakdown of waste.
- Temperature and moisture control: Composting is most efficient when the pile maintains adequate warmth and moisture. In colder climates, insulation might be necessary.
- Aeration: Mixing the composting material incorporates essential oxygen for aerobic decomposition and helps control odors.
- Emptying intervals: Depending on the system's design and the number of users, the composting chamber will need emptying anywhere from several times a year to once every few years.

While these tasks require a commitment, the routine quickly becomes a part of homestead life, like tending to a garden or caring for livestock.

Health and Safety Considerations

Handling human waste with care is crucial for health and safety. Here are essential guidelines to ensure your composting toilet system poses no risks:

- Use in non-edible gardens: To minimize health risks, apply the finished compost only to ornamental plants or trees, avoiding vegetable gardens.
- Compost maturation: The compost should be cured for at least a year after the last addition. This period ensures the breakdown of pathogens.
- Personal protection: Wear gloves and a mask when handling compost, and wash hands thoroughly afterward to prevent contamination.
- Regular monitoring: Look for signs of improper composting, such as persistent odors or flies, which may indicate the need for adjustments in moisture, aeration, or cover material.

By adhering to these practices, you can safely integrate a composting toilet into your homestead, contributing to a sustainable lifestyle that honors nature's cycles and conserves its resources.

Recycling and Repurposing Materials

In a world of finite resources, the ability to give new life to old items is a valuable skill for any homesteader. Recycling and repurposing go beyond sorting plastics and paper. The cornerstone of a sustainable homestead lies in viewing waste not as an endpoint but as the beginning of a new cycle. This perspective is rooted in two fundamental principles:

- Minimizing waste: At its heart, the drive to recycle and repurpose is about waste reduction. By finding new uses for materials, we decrease our consumption and, in turn, our environmental impact.
- Resource efficiency: This principle is about maximizing what we have. It involves seeing the potential in items beyond their initial purpose, thus extending their lifecycle and conserving the energy and materials needed to create new products.

Adhering to these principles supports the health of our planet and fosters a sense of ingenuity and resilience on the homestead.

Creative Repurposing Ideas

Viewing materials for their potential, rather than limiting them to their original purpose, opens up a world of creativity. Here are a few ideas to spark inspiration:

- Pallets into furniture: Wood pallets, often free, can be transformed into anything from benches to bookshelves.
- Glass jars as storage containers: Instead of buying new containers, clean glass jars from food products can be excellent vessels for storing grains, seeds, or homemade preserves.
- Old tires for garden beds: With some strategic cutting and painting, worn-out tires can become durable, raised garden beds for vegetables and flowers.
- Worn clothing into quilts or rags: Textiles that have seen better days can find new purposes as patchwork quilts or cleaning cloths, reducing the need for disposable products.

Along with reducing waste, these practices add a personal touch to the homestead, all while saving money.

Setting Up a Homestead Recycling System

An effective recycling system is pivotal for managing waste on the homestead. It involves several steps:

- Identify recyclable materials: Identify what is recyclable in your area, including plastics, metals, paper, and organic waste.
- Create sorting stations: Set up designated areas or bins for each type of recyclable material to simplify separating items as you use them.
- Educate household members: Make sure everyone in the home understands the sorting system and the importance of recycling, encouraging a shared commitment to these practices.
- Utilize composting: For organic waste, a compost system turns food scraps and yard waste into valuable fertilizer, closing the homestead's nutrient loop.

This structured approach not only simplifies recycling efforts but also ingrains these practices into the daily rhythm of homestead life.

Managing Farm and Garden Waste

The cycles of planting and harvesting generate a significant amount of organic waste, from crop residues to pruned branches. Rather than seeing this as a disposal challenge, view it as an opportunity for resourcefulness. Effective strategies include:

- Biochar: Transforming wood and other high-carbon waste into biochar through pyrolysis (burning in a low-oxygen environment) sequesters carbon, creating a potent soil amendment that improves nutrient retention and microbial life.
- Mulching: Using leaves, straw, or grass clippings as mulch not only suppresses weeds and conserves soil moisture but also breaks down over time, adding organic matter to the soil.
- Livestock feed: Many farm wastes, such as vegetable scraps or unsellable fruits, can supplement livestock diets, reducing feed costs.
- Green manure: Incorporating plant residues back into the soil as green manure adds nutrients and organic matter, enhancing soil fertility and structure.

Each of these practices turns potential waste into valuable assets that support the homestead's productivity and ecological balance.

Waste management exemplifies the core of sustainability for homesteaders, who see the end of a product's life as the start of a new one. By composting, repurposing, and employing similar methods, they treat waste not as a problem to solve but as a resource to utilize.

CREATING A RESILIENT HOMESTEAD LAYOUT

A thoughtful approach to laying out your homestead pays off in the short and long term, enhancing productivity, efficiency, and harmony with the natural world. The arrangement of buildings, gardens, and natural elements dictates the daily workflow and impacts the homestead's resilience to environmental challenges.

Strategic Placement of Buildings and Gardens

The thoughtful placement of structures and plantings is pivotal. Considerations include:

- Sunlight: Position buildings to maximize natural light while minimizing overheating. Gardens, especially vegetable plots, require ample sunlight, so place them in areas that receive consistent, direct daily exposure.
- Wind: Understanding prevailing wind patterns aids in placing windbreaks and designing buildings that can ventilate naturally during warmer months.
- Accessibility: Ensure that areas requiring frequent visits, like tool sheds or chicken coops, are easily accessible, reducing time and effort in daily chores.

This strategic approach enhances the efficiency of your homestead and contributes to energy conservation by reducing the need for artificial lighting and mechanical heating or cooling.

Incorporating Windbreaks and Shade

Trees and shrubbery serve as natural allies against the elements. By incorporating them thoughtfully, you can:

- Protect against wind: Strategic placement of trees can shield buildings and gardens from the harsh winds, potentially reducing heating costs and preventing soil erosion.
- Provide shade: In hotter climates, shade trees can significantly reduce temperatures, enhancing comfort and reducing the need for air conditioning. They can also protect sun-sensitive plants.

- Create microclimates: Trees and shrubs can modify local climates, creating more excellent, moist areas that support a wider variety of plants.

This natural infrastructure conserves energy and adds beauty and biodiversity to your homestead.

Designing for Biodiversity

Biodiversity is a cornerstone of ecological health, offering resilience against pests and diseases while supporting a rich web of life. To foster this diversity:

- Plant native species. They are adapted to the local climate and soil, require less maintenance, and offer habitat and food for native wildlife.
- Establish pollinator gardens: Flowers and plants that attract bees, butterflies, and other pollinators support these crucial species and enhance your garden's productivity.
- Create habitats: Features like ponds, brush piles, and rock walls offer refuge for various creatures, from frogs to beneficial insects and birds.

Emphasizing biodiversity creates a vibrant ecosystem where each element supports the others, contributing to a resilient and productive homestead.

Adapting to Climate Challenges:

Every homestead faces unique climate challenges, from drought and flooding to extreme temperatures. The water management and strategic placement strategies discussed in this chapter are your best tools for creating an adaptable landscape. For example, swales and rain gardens can mitigate flooding while recharging groundwater in regions with scarce rainfall at specific points of the year. In areas that experience wide temperature fluctuations, insulation and passive cooling can maintain comfortable year-round indoor temperatures with less energy invested in heating and cooling.

Learn about your region's climate challenges to anticipate and plan for them, ensuring your homestead's productivity and comfort throughout the seasons.

We've discussed a lot of concepts in this chapter, from the strategic placement of structures to the fostering of biodiversity and the adaptation to climate challenges. Each plays an integral part in building a homestead that is a place of personal refuge and a testament to sustainable living. Thoughtfulness and resilience guiding principles inform how we arrange our spaces and interact with the land, water, and life that share our landscape. Let these principles light the way as we shift gears from the foundational elements of design to the practical matters of building and cultivating your off-grid sanctuary.

4

CONSTRUCTING FOUNDATIONS:

BUILDING YOUR OFF-GRID HOME

Building a home in harmony with nature is a declaration of independence and sustainability in a world loud with modernity's noise. In this chapter, we'll create an off-grid home that balances practicality with aesthetics, efficiency with comfort, and innovation with tradition.

CHOOSING SUSTAINABLE BUILDING MATERIALS

The materials you choose lay the groundwork for the sustainability of your home. By selecting durable materials with a low environmental impact, you are not just building a home but also making a powerful choice to benefit the environment and your health. This empowering decision was made with materials such as:

- Bamboo: Rapidly renewable, sturdy, and versatile for flooring, framing, or furniture.

- Recycled Steel: Offers incredible strength with less material than wood framing, reducing the environmental footprint.
- Cob: A mixture of clay, sand, straw, and water, this ancient material is sustainable and provides excellent thermal mass.
- Straw bales: Used in walls, they provide outstanding insulation and use agricultural by-products.
- Hempcrete: A lighter, breathable alternative to concrete with good insulation.

When selecting from these materials, it's essential to consider what's available locally. This reduces transportation emissions and supports the local economy, making it a more sustainable and cost-effective choice.

ENERGY-EFFICIENT HOME DESIGN

Designing a home that minimizes energy use is a significant achievement. It's not just about building a structure but about creating a living space that works harmoniously with nature. Understanding the sun, wind, and local climate can help you determine the correct orientation. This can lead to a home that captures the sun's heat in the winter, reducing the need for artificial heating. This design achievement is something to be proud of.

Innovative use of insulation can also make a big difference here. You can control whether you're building from scratch or retrofitting an existing structure. Think of insulation as your home's sweater, providing an extra layer between the interior and the elements. High-quality insulation in the walls, roof, and floors will help maintain a consistent temperature across seasons and reduce the need for mechanical heating and cooling.

The placement and design of windows are a factor and can be used for summer cross-ventilation to cool your home naturally. Windows positioned for maximum natural lighting reduce the need for artificial lights, saving on electricity. The windows should be well-fitted, sealed, and insulated to minimize heat loss in the winter. Energy-efficient triple-pane designs will provide the best protection against temperature swings.

Understanding thermal mass is crucial. It's a property of certain materials, like stone or concrete, that allows them to absorb heat during the day and release it at night. This helps to regulate indoor temperatures and reduce the need for mechanical heating and cooling, an essential aspect of energy-efficient home design.

Incorporating these elements from the start is far more cost-effective and energy-efficient than trying to retrofit them later. However, if you've bought a property with an existing home, you can also improve the structure's energy efficiency.

Balancing Aesthetics and Functionality:

Your home should be a sanctuary that reflects your style while meeting practical needs. Achieving this balance is not just about design principles but creating a space that brings you joy and comfort. It involves integrating concepts such as:

- Open floor plans encourage natural light to permeate the space, facilitate heating and cooling, and offer flexibility.
- Natural finishes use wood, stone, or clay to add warmth and character to your home and blend well with the landscape.
- Outdoor living spaces utilizing patios, decks, or covered porches extend your living space into the outdoors, offering a seamless transition between inside and outside.

- Personal touches can make the space feel more "you," whether it's a bold color on a feature wall like a vibrant blue or a custom-built reading nook with a cozy window seat. You could also design a kitchen perfect for gatherings, with a large island and plenty of seating. These are just a few examples of personalizing your space to reflect your unique style and needs.

Remember, the most sustainable home is one that you love and want to keep living in for years to come. It's not just about ticking boxes for off-grid readiness. Your homestead should be a space that resonates with you on every level.

Every choice from foundation to roof has sustainability, efficiency, and personal well-being. Implications Whether selecting the materials that will form the bones of your home, designing the flow and function of spaces, or installing systems that ensure your independence from the grid, remember that each decision is a step towards creating a home that shelters, nourishes, and inspires.

DESIGNING AND CONSTRUCTING A GREENHOUSE

A greenhouse provides a controlled environment where plants can thrive away from the unpredictability of external conditions. Building a greenhouse is not merely about erecting a structure. It's a space with the power to extend the growing season, boost plant health, and increase yield. You'll need to find the optimal location and orientation, select appropriate materials, manage the internal climate, and integrate innovative growing systems such as aquaponics, which combines hydroponics and aquaculture, and hydroponics, a method of growing plants without soil. These systems can help you develop more food in less space and with less water, making your greenhouse even more sustainable.

Selecting the Right Location and Orientation

The site of your greenhouse will significantly influence its effectiveness. In the Northern Hemisphere, a south-facing location maximizes sunlight exposure, ensuring your plants receive ample light throughout the day. An east-west orientation of the longer sides maximizes solar gain during winter when the sun is low in the sky.

Along with light and sun exposure, there are other factors to consider. Putting the greenhouse near water sources allows for easier irrigation, but it's also important to consider water conservation. Collecting rainwater or using a drip irrigation system can help reduce water waste. If you live in a region prone to strong winds, protect the greenhouse from gusts that could cause damage or cool the interior too rapidly. Finally, consider the land underneath your greenhouse's foundation. Proper drainage will prevent water accumulation at its base that could erode the land or lead to other structural and foundation issues.

Greenhouse Styles and Materials

No style and material choice is ideal for everyone. Instead, the trick is to choose the right design for your budget, climate conditions, and aesthetic preferences. Let's start with the design style. There are two basic structures to choose from:

- Hoop House: Characterized by its semicircular shape, it is cost-effective and relatively easy to construct. It is made of metal hoops covered with plastic sheeting and is ideal for seasonal extension.
- Geodesic Dome: This spherical structure offers excellent strength against wind and snow loads. Its unique shape allows for even light distribution but can be more complex and costly to build.

The second part of this question is what materials you'll use for the walls and roof of your greenhouse. There are three primary material choices:

- Glass: Traditional and visually appealing, glass offers excellent light transmission but can be expensive and fragile. It also may require shading to prevent overheating.
- Polycarbonate: Durable, lightweight, and providing sound and light diffusion, polycarbonate panels are an energy-efficient choice, though they may yellow over time.
- Greenhouse Plastic: Polyethylene or polyvinyl covers are the most affordable options. They provide sound light transmission and are easy to replace but have a shorter lifespan than rigid materials.

Consider your budget and your property when deciding on the combination of style and materials you'll use. Also, remember that a higher price doesn't always translate to a better choice. Glass may not be the best option for your greenhouse if there's a lack of shade. A plastic or polycarbonate structure will likely be more affordable and provide a better growing environment.

Climate Control in Greenhouses

Creating and maintaining optimal growing conditions within your greenhouse involves managing temperature, humidity, and ventilation.

- Temperature: To maintain a consistent climate, use automatic vent openers that respond to temperature changes. During colder months, use thermal mass, like water barrels painted black and placed where they can absorb sunlight, to improve heat retention.

- Humidity: Adequate ventilation controls moisture and prevents plant diseases. Consider installing roof and side vents or using a fan system to circulate air.
- Ventilation: Manual or automatic venting systems allow for adjusting internal conditions. Mesh screens on vents keep pests out while allowing airflow.

Monitoring these elements ensures plants grow in an environment tailored to their needs, promoting optimal health and productivity.

Incorporating Aquaponics and Hydroponics

Embracing aquaponics or hydroponics within your greenhouse design introduces a soil-less cultivation method that can significantly increase efficiency and yield. These closely related concepts differ slightly in their application:

- Aquaponics: This system combines aquaculture (raising fish) with hydroponics (growing plants in water) in a symbiotic environment. Fish waste provides an organic nutrient source for the plants, while the plants naturally filter and clean the water, which is then recirculated back to the fish. Setting up an aquaponics system requires careful planning to balance the needs of plants and fish. Still, the result is a highly productive, water-efficient growing method that promotes a deeper understanding of ecological relationships and the closed-loop systems that define sustainable living.
- Hydroponics: Hydroponics involves growing plants in nutrient-rich water without soil. This method allows precise control over nutrient levels and significantly increases growth rates and yields. Various hydroponic systems exist, from simple wick systems to more complex drip or aeroponic systems. Each has advantages and

suitability for different types of plants or space constraints within the greenhouse.

With careful planning and management, aquaponics and hydroponics can transform your greenhouse into a year-round food production powerhouse, embodying the principles of efficiency and self-sufficiency central to off-grid homesteading.

ESSENTIAL OUTBUILDINGS FOR STORAGE AND TOOLS

Outbuildings are the unsung heroes of a well-organized homestead, quietly ensuring that every tool and supply has its place. From the humble shed that guards your gardening implements against the elements to the barn that keeps your harvests safe and dry, these structures play a pivotal role in the smooth operation of your off-grid life. Here, we'll assess your storage needs, construct and organize outbuildings for maximum efficiency, and protect them against common adversaries like pests and inclement weather.

Planning Your Storage Needs

Start by taking stock of what you have and what you anticipate needing in terms of storage. Categories might include:

- Tools: From hand tools to power tools and everything in between, consider the volume, size, and special storage requirements (like climate control for specific power tools).
- Equipment: Larger items such as tractors, tillers, and mowers demand more spacious accommodations.
- Harvests: Think about the quantity of produce, grains, or other goods you expect to store and any specific

conditions they require, like ventilation for garlic or excellent storage for root vegetables.
- Supplies: This can encompass everything from animal feed to canning jars and gardening pots.

Reflecting on these categories helps determine the size and type of outbuildings you need. A tool shed, for instance, requires different considerations than a barn intended for storing large equipment or harvests.

DIY Shed and Outbuilding Construction

Constructing your outbuildings can be broken down into five big-picture steps:

1. Design: Draft a plan that accommodates all your storage needs while considering future growth. Also, consider what materials you'll use and their environmental impact. For instance, using materials like reclaimed wood or local stone centers is sustainable in your outbuilding construction.
2. Foundation: Common foundation types include concrete, gravel, and pier blocks. The structure's size, purpose, and composition of the land it will be built will help guide you to the right choice for your property.
3. Frame: Erect the frame, ensuring it's sturdy and level. Timber framing is often sufficient for smaller sheds, while larger structures may require a more robust frame.
4. Roof and Walls: Install the ceiling and walls, incorporating natural light sources such as skylights or translucent panels to reduce the need for artificial lighting.
5. Finishing Touches: Add doors, shelves, hooks, and other organizational features. Natural finishes like linseed oil

can protect wood frames and walls without harming the environment.

Organizing for Efficiency

A well-organized outbuilding saves time and prevents frustration. Once the basic structure has been constructed, take a moment to plan and visualize what you'll store there before you install shelves or assign a spot for each item. The things you use the most should be placed in the most accessible areas so you can quickly grab what you need. More specialized or less-used supplies can go on higher shelves or rear areas that keep them safe and out of the way until you need them.

Full use of your outbuildings means thinking in three dimensions: horizontal and vertical space. Shelving is the most common way to do this. You can also use wall—or ceiling-mounted hooks or magnetic strips to store tools off the floor and keep them easily accessible.

Creating zones for different categories of items can also be an effective way to streamline your workflow. For example, you may have one area for gardening tools, another for woodworking supplies, and a third for animal care products. Dividing the space into these quadrants before you move in any supplies lets you tailor the shelving and storage options in each zone to match the tools you'll keep there.

Use labels smartly once you've determined your storage zones and installed shelving. This simple step can make a big difference in keeping things ordered and finding precisely what you need when you need it. Along with labeling shelves or hooks, ensure that any bins or drawers are appropriately labeled with what they contain, especially if they're opaque.

Finally, remember that your storage needs may change over time. Periodically review what's stored in your outbuildings. Consider whether reassigning the zones within the space would improve your workflow. If there are items you haven't used in a while, it may be time to donate or discard them to prevent clutter.

Securing Outbuildings Against Pests and Weather

Protection against pests and weather not only safeguards your tools and supplies but also extends the life of the outbuilding itself. Some of the critical areas to consider in this regard include:

- Pest Control: Seal gaps and cracks where rodents or insects might enter. For added defense, use natural deterrents like diatomaceous earth around the perimeter.
- Weatherproofing: Choose materials that stand up to the unique challenges presented by your local climate, whether that's heavy snow loads or intense sun. Proper insulation and ventilation keep the interior dry and prevent mold or mildew regardless of climate.
- Roof Maintenance: Regularly inspect and maintain the roof to prevent leaks. Trim overhanging branches to minimize debris and moisture retention.
- Foundation Care: Ensure the area around the foundation remains well-drained to avoid water damage. Proper grading and gutters can direct water away from the structure.

A thoughtfully planned and organized system of outbuildings creates a network of spaces that contribute to your homestead's overall efficiency and sustainability. In their simplicity and utility, these structures become integral to the daily rhythm of off-grid life, crafting a functional space in tune with the natural environment.

ANIMAL HOUSING: FROM COOPS TO BARNS

Creating a haven for livestock on your homestead goes beyond mere shelter from the elements. These environments should cater to the unique needs of each animal, ensuring their health, safety, and happiness. The design and construction of animal housing such as coops, barns, and hutches must consider the specific requirements of chickens, goats, rabbits, and other livestock you plan to raise. This careful planning contributes to your animals' well-being and your homestead's efficiency and productivity.

Chapter 6 provides more in-depth advice on creating spaces suited to specific animals. For now, let's take a big-picture overview of how to build structures on your property designed to meet the needs of your animal populations.

Designing for Different Livestock Needs

Each type of livestock comes with its own set of housing needs, influenced by its behavior, size, and the role it plays on your homestead:

- Chickens: Coops for chickens should provide adequate space for roosting and nesting. The recommended allowance is 2-3 square feet per chicken inside the coop and 8-10 square feet in an outside run. The airflow in the coop should strike a balance, providing enough ventilation to prevent respiratory issues while avoiding drafts. Include predator-proofing measures like secure latches and wire mesh buried around the perimeter.
- Goats: Goats require sturdy, draft-free barns or sheds with ample space for exercise and play. A good rule of thumb is to provide a minimum of 15-20 square feet per goat inside the shelter. Fencing must be strong and tall enough to

prevent escapes, and you should provide adequate shelter from rain and cold weather. Goats also benefit from structures to climb on, satisfying their instincts.

- Rabbits: Rabbit hutches or colonies need protection from predators and extreme weather, with enough room for rabbits to move freely. Each rabbit requires about 12 square feet of space. Elevate the cabinets to make them easier to clean. Providing a nesting box within the hutch offers a secluded spot for rabbits to rest or raise their kits.

Considering the specific needs of each species when designing animal housing ensures not only the comfort, health, and safety of your livestock but also their long-term productivity, whether in the form of eggs, milk, meat, or wool.

Sustainable Construction Techniques

Using sustainable techniques in the construction of animal shelters reduces your environmental footprint, aligns with the ethos of off-grid homesteading–and is cost-effective, to boot. Use reclaimed or locally sourced materials whenever possible. Old barn wood, pallets, and stones can be repurposed into beautiful, functional structures. Consider natural building methods like cob or straw bale construction for larger shelters. These methods provide excellent insulation and reduce the need for heating or cooling.

Another excellent option is to use green roofs or living roofs on structures like chicken coops or rabbit hutches. These offer additional insulation, reduce runoff, and blend structures into the landscape.

These approaches contribute to the sustainability of your homestead by creating animal housing that is both functional and harmonious with the surrounding environment.

Maintaining Healthy Living Conditions

Regular maintenance of animal housing is essential to prevent disease and ensure a clean, safe environment for your livestock. Establish a routine cleaning schedule to remove manure, refresh bedding, and disinfect waterers and feeders to prevent ammonia buildup and reduce disease risk.

Along with keeping the interior clean, inspect structures regularly for signs of wear, damage, or potential entry points for predators. Prompt repairs safeguard your animals and the longevity of the housing. Pay particular attention to ventilation points, ensuring they're clear of obstructions and allow fresh airflow while avoiding drafts, particularly in colder months.

These maintenance practices support the well-being of your animals and contribute to your homestead's overall health.

Integrating Animal Areas with Gardens

Positioning animal housing and runs adjacent to or within your garden areas can offer mutual benefits, creating a synergistic relationship between livestock and plant cultivation. Examples of intelligent animal integration include:

- Placing chicken coops near gardens allows easy manure transfer to compost piles, enriching garden soil with valuable nutrients.
- Rotating grazing areas for goats or chickens are utilized to clear and fertilize fallow sections of the garden, preparing them for planting.
- Keeping rabbits adjacent to vegetable gardens where they can benefit from garden trimmings as part of their diet. Rabbit manure also doesn't require composting and can be directly applied to garden beds.

Thoughtful integration of animals into growing areas maximizes the efficiency of your homestead by cycling nutrients and managing pests naturally. The result is a living system where each element supports and enhances the others, embodying the harmony of living things with their environment at the heart of off-grid homesteading.

5

NURTURING YOUR LAND:

THE ART OF CROP SELECTION

Living in harmony with nature means using the resources available on your land to provide for your family's needs. Choosing suitable crops for your climate supports this goal because you won't need to fight against the natural weather conditions to get your crops to thrive. They'll be naturally inclined to survive in your landscape–all you'll need to do is provide the nourishment and protection to set them up for success. The process of choosing crops that align with your environment can be complex. Still, it is a challenge worth the effort to overcome, enhancing the resilience and productivity of your homestead.

UNDERSTANDING YOUR GROWING ZONE

The USDA Hardiness Zone Map is a crucial tool for gardeners. It delineates regions based on their average annual minimum winter temperature. Once you know your zone, this can act as a compass, guiding your crop selection to ensure your garden's success. For example, a gardener in Zone 5 would fare well with cold-tolerant crops like kale and brussel sprouts, while someone in Zone 9 might focus on heat-loving plants like peppers and eggplant.

The USDA website is the most accessible place for most to find the Hardiness Zone Map. You can also consult gardening books to find your zone. These zones are relatively broad, so it can also be helpful to supplement this knowledge with input from your local community. Neighbors who are experienced gardeners can give you insights into specific crops that tend to do well in your area or ones that they've struggled to cultivate, further refining your crop selection.

Consider the broader USDA zones and the microclimates on your property. Factors such as landscape layout and sunlight exposure can generate pockets of warmth or coolness, influencing which crops thrive beyond the typical zone recommendations. Identifying these microclimates expands your crop options and helps you strategically position plants for optimal growth and productivity.

Selecting Climate-appropriate Vegetables and Fruits

When choosing plants well-suited to your climate, you don't need to try as hard to keep them alive. Instead, you can focus on ensuring they flourish and produce bountiful harvests.

Start by researching what grows well in your area. Incorporating native plants into your garden supports local ecosystems and wildlife. Many local plants will also naturally resist local pests or diseases.

In addition, consider planting heirloom varieties. These are often adapted to specific climates, providing an extra level of natural resilience (and they'll usually taste better, too).

Adapting to Microclimates on Your Homestead

Every piece of land is a mosaic of microclimates, small areas where the climate differs from the surrounding land. For example, you may have a south-facing wall that radiates heat, creating a warm microclimate perfect for tomatoes. Or there's a shaded spot where cooler-temperature crops can extend their season.

The first step to identifying your property's microclimates is to observe the land and record what you see. Keep a garden journal noting temperature differences and how plants respond in different areas. From there, you can experiment with crops that may not typically thrive in your zone. Consider adding a trellis for shade or using reflective mulches to increase sunlight, which can make a surprising difference, maximizing the use of existing microclimates.

SOIL PREPARATION AND NATURAL FERTILIZERS

The foundation of a productive garden lies not in the seeds we sow but in the soil we nurture. Soil, brimming with life, is the bedrock of our gardens, supporting plant growth and the health of the entire ecosystem. By blending age-old practices with modern insights, you can cultivate fertile, living soil and foster an environment where plants can flourish.

Building Healthy Soil

Soil is a complex, living entity that requires care and attention. There's more to cultivating healthy soil than just adding nutrients. A vibrant ecosystem exists below the surface, and its health is paramount to support the plants that grow above. Some strategies to maintain soil health include:

- Composting: Composting transforms kitchen scraps, yard waste, and other organic materials into rich, nutrient-dense humus. This black gold feeds the soil and improves its structure, increasing its ability to retain moisture and oxygen.
- Mulching: A layer of mulch, straw, leaves, or wood chips acts as a protective blanket for the soil. It conserves moisture, suppresses weeds, and feeds the soil as it decomposes, enhancing its fertility.
- No-till gardening: Tilling the soil can disrupt its natural structure and harm the organisms that call it home. A no-till approach preserves these soil ecosystems, reducing erosion and improving water retention.

DIY Natural Fertilizers

Commercial fertilizers, while convenient, can carry a high environmental cost. Creating natural fertilizers is an accessible and sustainable alternative, turning what might be waste into a valuable resource for your garden. Some popular natural fertilizer options include:

- Compost tea: Steep compost in water to create a nutrient-rich liquid that gives plants a quick energy boost.
- Manure tea: Like compost tea, manure tea uses aged livestock manure. It's a potent fertilizer; use it sparingly to avoid burning plants.
- Eggshell and coffee ground fertilizer: Crushed eggshells provide calcium, while coffee grounds offer nitrogen. Mixed into the soil, they can improve plant health and deter pests.

- Banana peel fertilizer: Rich in potassium, soaking banana peels in water creates a simple, effective fertilizer for flowering and fruiting plants.

These homemade options reduce waste and ensure your garden receives a balanced diet tailored to its needs.

Testing and Amending Soil

Understanding the composition of your soil is akin to unlocking a secret language that will tell you the needs and potential of your garden. You can gain a wealth of information about soil health from conducting simple tests such as:

- Nutrient tests: Affordable testing kits available at garden centers can reveal the levels of crucial nutrients, guiding your fertilization strategy.
- pH testing: The acidity or alkalinity of your soil affects nutrient availability. A pH test can help you adjust your soil's pH level using natural amendments like sulfur or lime to create the ideal plant-growing environment.
- Texture and structure analysis: Observing how soil holds water or forms into clumps can indicate its texture and structure, suggesting amendments like sand for drainage or compost for moisture retention.

With this knowledge, you can take a more precise and scientific approach to amending your soil, ensuring you create the perfect foundation for plant growth.

Cover Crops for Soil Health

Cover crops are a gardener's ally in maintaining and enhancing soil health and offer numerous benefits if planted during off-seasons:

- Nitrogen fixation: Legumes, such as clover and vetch, capture nitrogen from the air, enriching the soil for future crops.
- Erosion prevention: Cover crops protect the soil from erosion by rain and wind, preserving its structure and nutrients.
- Weed suppression: Fast-growing cover crops can outcompete weeds, reducing the need for manual weeding.
- Soil structure improvement: The roots of cover crops break up compacted soil, improving aeration and water infiltration.

Incorporating cover crops into your garden rotation nurtures the soil and sets the stage for more abundant, healthier harvests in the coming seasons.

Preparing and enriching the soil is a gesture of respect and recognition of the soil's vital role in the web of life. We pay homage to the decay and renewal cycles fueling our gardens through composting, mulching, and the thoughtful use of natural fertilizers. Testing, soil amendment, and planting cover crops are further forms of ecological stewardship, ensuring bountiful gardens and nurturing the unseen life that makes growth possible.

COMPANION PLANTING AND CROP ROTATION

Every plant in a thriving garden contributes to the health and productivity of its neighbors. This interconnectedness is at the heart of companion planting, which pairs different crops to enhance growth, deter pests, and improve pollination. Similarly, crop rotation maintains the delicate balance of soil health, disrupting the cycles of pests and diseases while preventing nutrient depletion. Together, these strategies ensure the vitality of your garden ecosystem.

Principles of Companion Planting

Companion planting operates on the principle of symbiotic relationships, with each contributing to the other's well-being. Some plants emit natural pest-repellent substances, reducing the need for chemical interventions, while others, mainly flowering plants, attract beneficial insects that aid in pollination. Specific pairings can improve nutrient uptake and even enhance the flavor of their garden companions. For instance, legumes fix nitrogen in the soil, making them ideal companions for nitrogen-hungry plants such as tomatoes and cucumbers.

Successful Companion Planting Pairs

Identifying the right plant pairs is pivotal for a harmonious garden. Below are examples of companion planting pairs and the logic behind their compatibility:

- Tomatoes and basil: Basil repels flies and mosquitoes while potentially enhancing the flavor of tomatoes.
- Carrots and onions: The strong scent of onions can deter carrot flies, protecting the crop.
- Cucumbers and nasturtiums: Nasturtiums act as a trap crop for cucumber beetles while adding a splash of color to the garden.
- Corn, beans, and squash: Known as the "Three Sisters," this trio supports each other—corn provides a structure for beans to climb, beans fix nitrogen in the soil, and squash shades the ground, reducing weed growth.

Incorporating these pairs into your garden plan optimizes your crops' health and yield and fosters a vibrant, self-sustaining garden ecosystem.

Crop Rotation

Rotating crops from one season or year to the next is crucial in maintaining soil health and fertility. This practice has numerous benefits. First, changing the type of crop grown in a particular garden area can prevent the depletion of specific nutrients. Second, rotating heavy feeders with light or nitrogen-fixing plants helps maintain soil fertility.

Rotating crops also helps break the life cycles of plant-specific pests and diseases. Changing the crops grown in an area prevents these organisms from establishing a permanent foothold.

There are benefits to crop rotation beneath the surface, too. The root systems of different plants affect soil structure in various ways. Alternating deep and Shallow-rooted plants can prevent soil compaction and promote healthy root growth.

Planning Your Garden Layout

A well-thought-out garden layout incorporating companion planting and crop rotation is critical to maximizing your garden's health and productivity. Consider the following strategies when planning your layout:

- Group compatible plants: Arrange your garden so companion plants are neighbors, taking advantage of their mutual benefits.
- Map out a rotation plan: Divide your garden into sections and rotate the types of crops grown in each section annually. Keeping a garden journal can help track what was planted, where, and when.

- Consider plant families: To simplify crop rotation, group plants by their families, as members of the same family often have similar nutrient needs and attract the same pests.

Implementing these strategies requires some foresight and planning, but the reward for this effort is a garden brimming with life that yields bountiful harvests. By embracing the principles of companion planting and crop rotation, you enhance your garden's vitality and create a legacy of abundance and health for the seasons to come.

NATURAL PEST CONTROL METHODS

One big question that many new homesteaders have is how to manage garden pests to maintain the harmony between human activity and natural ecosystems. The good news is that you don't need to rely on chemical pesticides and other harmful, invasive approaches to keep your crops healthy. Pests have natural predators, and attracting them can protect your garden in a way that supports, rather than disrupts, the natural ecosystem of your land. You can also utilize natural deterrents and implement Integrated Pest Management strategies to preserve the health and vibrancy of your garden without compromising the integrity of the environment.

Identifying Common Garden Pests

Recognizing potential pests is the first step to managing them. This knowledge not only aids in early detection but also helps in understanding the ecological role these creatures play, allowing for more informed decisions regarding control measures. For instance:

- Aphids: Small, pear-shaped insects that cluster on the undersides of leaves, sucking sap and weakening plants. While troublesome, they are a food source for ladybugs.
- Cabbage worms: These green caterpillars blend in with the foliage of brassicas, consuming leaves and leaving behind skeletal remains.
- Tomato hornworms are large, green caterpillars with horn-like tails. They feed on tomato plants but are frequently targeted by helpful braconid wasps for parasitization.

Familiarize yourself with each pest's lifecycle and habits. This knowledge will help you develop effective control strategies.

DIY Pest Control Solutions

Crafting your pest control solutions reduces reliance on chemical pesticides and ensures the safety of beneficial insects and the broader ecosystem. Here are some recipes and methods that have proven effective:

- Garlic pepper spray strongly deters pests. It combines garlic, hot peppers, a dash of soap, and water.
- Neem oil, extracted from the neem tree, interrupts pests' life cycles when spread on leaves, serving as a natural repellent.
- Diatomaceous earth, a powder made from fossilized algae, can be scattered around plant bases to ward off slugs and other soft-bodied pests.

When used judiciously, these solutions offer a first line of defense, safeguarding your plants while maintaining the ecological balance of your garden.

Encouraging Beneficial Predators

One of the most effective ways to control pests is to outsource the work to birds, bats, and insects that feed on them. This approach is a win-win, reducing pest populations while contributing to the biodiversity of your homestead. To support these natural allies:

- Plant a pollinator garden: Flowers such as lavender, yarrow, and marigold attract predatory insects like ladybugs and lacewings, which feast on aphids and other pests.
- Install birdhouses and bat boxes: Birds and bats are voracious consumers of insects. Providing shelter for these creatures encourages them to reside near your garden, offering natural pest control.
- Create a pond: A small garden can attract frogs and dragonflies, which help control mosquito populations and other pests.

Fostering an environment that welcomes natural predators can significantly reduce the need for manual pest intervention, allowing nature to protect your garden.

Integrated Pest Management (IPM) Strategies

Integrated Pest Management (IPM) is a holistic approach to pest control that emphasizes the least possible hazard to people, property, and the environment. IPM strategies involve:

- Monitoring and identification: Regularly inspect your garden for signs of pests. Once you identify them, you can tailor your control methods effectively.
- Preventive cultural practices: Healthy plants are less likely to succumb to pests. Crop rotation, proper spacing, and

adequate watering and fertilization are all preventive measures that strengthen plant health.
- Mechanical controls: Physical barriers like row covers or traps can prevent pests from reaching plants. Handpicking larger pests like hornworms is also effective.
- Biological control: Introducing or encouraging natural predators and parasitoids can help manage pest populations without chemical interventions.

IPM is not a single action but a series of decisions and practices that work together to create a robust defense against garden pests. It's about maintaining a natural balance and preventing crop problems while minimizing environmental impact.

Embracing natural pest control methods aligns your gardening practices with the broader principles of respect for nature and a commitment to leaving a light footprint on the earth. You can protect your gardens from pests through thoughtful observation and creative solutions while nurturing the delicate ecological balance that sustains us all.

SEASON EXTENSION TECHNIQUES: FROM GREENHOUSES TO COLD FRAMES

Extending the growing season transforms a short-lived summer harvest into a continuous abundance throughout the year, which increases yields and broadens the range of crops you can cultivate. As a result, you maintain a consistent flow of fresh produce regardless of the season.

With a few clever strategies, your garden can produce fresh vegetables far beyond the traditional growing season, offering fresh greens in the fall and early tomatoes in the spring.

Chapter 4 discussed one common strategy for doing this: greenhouses. While these can be an investment, a greenhouse offers the most control over the growing environment, allowing for a wide range of crops year-round.

A more straightforward and more affordable strategy is to utilize cold frames. These are bottomless boxes with a transparent lid that traps heat and protects plants from frost. They can be made from repurposed materials like old windows to make them more sustainable and cost-effective.

Hoop houses, plastic tunnel-like structures, step up from cold frames. They offer more space for plants and easier access for gardeners.

For those looking to extend their growing season, these techniques provide a way to enjoy fresh produce throughout the year and offer the joy of gardening even as the snow falls.

Using Greenhouses Effectively

Greenhouses provide a controlled environment where warmth and humidity are maintained, allowing for a thriving garden even when the landscape outside is barren. The key to a successful greenhouse lies in its design and management.

Firstly, location is critical. Position your greenhouse to maximize sunlight exposure, ideally with a south-facing orientation. While full sun is beneficial in the winter, it may prove too aggressive in the summer, resulting in scorched plants. Shading can prevent this. You can use external shading nets for a temporary, seasonal solution or apply internal shading paints if you need them all year.

Ventilation and insulation are also essential for regulating temperature and preventing overheating during warmer months. Automated roof vents can provide a hands-free approach to managing this balance. Insulation can be applied to retain heat in the winter, and there are some DIY strategies you can employ in this area. For instance, bubble wrap can be an inexpensive solution to line the interior of your greenhouse without obstructing light.

By tailoring these elements to your specific climate and crop needs, your greenhouse becomes an engine of year-round plant productivity.

Cold Frames for Early Starts and Late Harvests

Cold frames, essentially mini-greenhouses, offer a more straightforward way to protect your plants from frost. They give them a head start in spring and extend growth into the colder months.

The construction of cold frames can be as straightforward as repurposing old windows atop a wooden box frame. The key is ensuring the top is angled to catch the sun and adequate drainage.

Once constructed, place the cold frames in a sunny, sheltered spot in your garden to maximize warmth and light. Prop open the lid on sunny days to prevent overheating, then close it at night to retain the heat from the day.

Incorporating cold frames into your garden setup is a low-cost, highly effective method to extend your growing season. They offer a gentle, nurturing space for seedlings to grow or for hardier greens to thrive in the chill of winter.

Other Season Extension Techniques

Beyond greenhouses and cold frames, there are different methods to shield your crops from the cold, each of which offers a unique blend of protection and ease of use:

- Row covers: Lightweight fabrics laid directly over crops can protect them from frost, allowing light and moisture to penetrate them. They can also be easily removed as temperatures rise.
- Thermal mass: Objects like water barrels painted black and placed in a greenhouse can absorb heat during the day and release it at night, moderating temperature fluctuations.
- Heat sinks: Like thermal mass, heat sinks, such as stone or concrete floors, can absorb heat and reradiate it into the environment, providing a steady source of warmth.
- Mulching: Applying a thick layer of mulch around plants can insulate the soil, keeping root systems warmer and extending the growing period.

By integrating these techniques, you create a bulwark against the cold, turning even the most inhospitable seasons into opportunities for growth.

The bottom line is that the limits of the growing season are more flexible than they seem. By intelligently applying greenhouses, cold frames, and other innovative methods, you can coax more life from the earth and enjoy the fruits and vegetables of your labor throughout the year.

6

RAISING THE HOMESTEAD:

A GUIDE TO LIVESTOCK CARE

Imagine the sound of chickens clucking in the background as you tend to your garden chores, the sight of goats playfully headbutting each other in the field, or the quiet hum of bees busy at work in their hives. These are not just idyllic scenes from a pastoral fantasy but tangible aspects of life on an off-grid homestead. Livestock provides more than just food or products; it contributes to the homestead's life cycle, offering companionship, waste recycling, and garden pest control. However, diving into animal husbandry without a clear understanding of the responsibilities and care required can lead to more than just a few ruffled feathers. This chapter lays the groundwork for integrating livestock into your homestead, focusing on animal care, behavior, and health management essentials.

CHOOSING THE RIGHT LIVESTOCK FOR YOUR HOMESTEAD

Only some types of livestock will fit every homestead. Matchmaking is required to choose animals compatible with your homestead, lifestyle, and goals. Here are vital factors to consider:

- Space: Each animal has spatial requirements for roaming, grazing, and shelter. Chickens can thrive in smaller spaces, while goats and pigs need more room to roam.
- Feed: Assess the availability and cost of feed in your area and the potential to produce your own. Goats, for instance, can help with weed control, turning what might be a chore into a beneficial activity.
- Care needs: Every animal demands a certain level of care, from daily feeding and clean water provision to more specific needs like shearing or milking.

PRIMARY CARE AND FEEDING

Properly dieting your livestock is the cornerstone of their health and well-being. It starts with understanding the dietary needs of each species. For example, chickens require a balanced diet of grains, proteins, and greens supplemented with kitchen scraps and garden waste. As browsers rather than grazers, goats prefer to eat leaves, twigs, and shrubs, making them excellent natural landscapers.

Providing your livestock with a proper diet starts by researching their nutritional needs and the feed options you have available to meet them. Once you've solidified the "what" of their diet, the next step is the "when." Regular feeding times establish a routine that can help you more efficiently manage your livestock and promote animal health by ensuring they have steady access to proper nutrition.

Clean, accessible water is another vital ingredient for healthy, happy livestock. It can be as simple as a trough or bowl within the pen that you fill manually or a more involved system plumbed directly into your water supply to refill automatically.

The last major piece of this puzzle is a shelter that protects your animals from the elements and predators. The proper shelter depends on the local climate and the animal's needs. You can find more information on constructing animal shelters in Chapter 4.

UNDERSTANDING ANIMAL BEHAVIOR

Understanding animal behavior is necessary for effective management and care and can also be a source of fascination and joy. Just like people, animals have personalities. For example, chickens establish a 'pecking order,' which can influence feeding arrangements and coop dynamics. Conversely, goats are curious and playful but can also be escape artists, requiring secure fencing. Observing and learning these behaviors allows for a more harmonious homestead where your animals' needs and natural tendencies are respected and accommodated.

HEALTH AND WELLNESS CHECKS

Regular health checks are a cornerstone of maintaining animal health and the vitality of your homestead. They aid in early detection and prevention of health issues by monitoring for signs of illness or distress, maintaining a vaccination and deworming schedule, and promptly and adequately treating injuries. For instance, limping in a goat could indicate hoof problems, which are common and addressed through regular trimming and care.

Establishing a relationship with a veterinarian experienced with your types of livestock is a crucial step in your livestock care journey. They can examine the animals to get a baseline health reading, which will aid in the diagnosis of potential health issues down the line. A trusted professional gives you peace of mind and supports you when needed, ensuring the health and well-being of your livestock.

Nurturing the animals that share your homestead is not just a duty but a way to build a relationship based on mutual respect, care, and understanding. Their well-being directly influences the vitality of the homestead itself, so properly caring for the animals on your property benefits everyone. You can ensure that your livestock thrives as part of your extended family through thoughtful selection, attentive care, and a keen eye for their health and happiness.

CHICKENS: BREEDS, CARE, AND EGG PRODUCTION

Raising chickens is fulfilling, and the relatively small space they require makes them a popular choice for homesteaders. They offer a source of fresh eggs, companionship, and natural pest control. The key to a thriving flock is understanding the nuances of breed selection, habitat creation, nutritional needs, and strategies to enhance egg production.

Selecting Chicken Breeds

The diversity among chicken breeds is vast, and each breed has strengths. Some excel in egg production, while others are prized for their meat yield or adaptability. Broadly, chickens fall into three categories:

- Egg-laying breeds: Known for their prolific egg production, breeds like the Leghorn or Sussex can provide a steady supply of eggs. They are typically lighter in weight and more active.
- Meat breeds: Bred for rapid growth and substantial meat yield, meat breeds such as the Cornish Cross are larger and have a shorter lifespan. Due to their size, they require more feed and space.
- Dual-purpose breeds: Breeds like the Plymouth Rock or Rhode Island Red offer versatility for homesteaders looking for both. They are hardy and well-suited to various climates, balancing egg production with meat yield.

Making the correct choice involves considering your homestead's goals, space, and climate. For those just starting, dual-purpose breeds often provide a balanced introduction to chicken keeping and are adaptable to egg production and meat.

Designing a Chicken Coop and Run

The ideal living space for chickens mimics their natural tendencies towards roosting and foraging, ensuring their health and happiness. Essential elements include:

- Space: Allocate at least 3 square feet per chicken inside the coop and 10 square feet in the run. Overcrowding can lead to stress and health issues.
- Ventilation: Proper airflow is critical to remove moisture and ammonia, keeping the air fresh and reducing the risk of respiratory problems.
- Protection: Secure the coop and run against predators with sturdy construction and hardware cloth. Consider an elevated coop to deter ground predators.

- Nesting boxes: Provide one nesting box for every 3-4 hens, filled with soft bedding to encourage egg-laying.

Along with incorporating these features, make sure your coop and run are easily accessible for humans when it's time to clean and collect eggs.

Feeding and Caring for Chickens

Nutrition plays a pivotal role in the health and productivity of your chickens. A balanced diet consists of:

- Layer feed: Formulated for egg-laying breeds, it contains protein and calcium to support shell formation and overall health.
- Grit: Chi requires grit to help digest their food, acting as teeth in other animals.
- Supplements: Oyster shell as a calcium supplement can be offered separately for laying hens to ensure strong eggshells.
- Freshwater: A constant supply of readily accessible and clean water is essential, especially in hot weather or for laying hens.

There are some other steps you can take, beyond seeing to their nutritional needs, to ensure the health of your flock. Conduct regular health checks for parasites, injuries, or other issues. You can prevent many health concerns by maintaining clean living conditions within the coop and run. Providing enrichment, such as perches or dust baths, is another step to contribute to a healthy, productive flock.

Maximizing Egg Production

For many homesteaders, eggs are a primary reason for raising chickens. Enhancing egg production involves:

- Breed selection: Opt for high-producing egg breeds if egg quantity is your goal. Research and choose breeds known for their laying capabilities.
- Lighting: Egg production can decrease during shorter winter days. Supplemental light in the coop can help maintain production - aim for 14-16 hours of light daily if egg production is your primary goal.
- Nutrition: High-quality layer feed and access to fresh water are non-negotiable for optimal egg production. Nutritional deficiencies can quickly decrease laying.
- Stress reduction: A calm and stable environment supports consistent egg-laying. Minimize changes in their routine and environment to avoid stress-induced drops in production.

By focusing on these critical areas, you set the stage for a flock that not only thrives but also significantly contributes to your homestead's self-sufficiency.

GOATS FOR MILK, MEAT, AND LAND MANAGEMENT

Goats offer more to a homestead than just their endearing personalities. These versatile animals bring many benefits, from the practicality of milk and meat production to their natural prowess in controlling weeds. Their adaptability and relatively low maintenance make them an excellent choice for both seasoned homesteaders and those new to the lifestyle.

Goats have earned a reputation as efficient land managers and excel in weed control. They happily graze on many types of vegetation that other livestock might avoid, keeping your land clear and reducing the need for chemical herbicides while fostering a more organic environment. Furthermore, goats produce milk that is easier to digest than cow's milk due to its smaller fat globules. For those considering meat production, goats provide a leaner option, with various breeds suited to different climatic conditions and preferences.

Creating a secure living space for goats is paramount to their well-being and your peace of mind. Goats are known for their Houdini-like escape skills, making robust fencing a must. A combination of sturdy posts and wire mesh, standing at least 4 feet high, typically suffices to keep goats contained. Their housing should also offer protection from the elements, with well-ventilated, draft-free shelters where they can retreat during inclement weather. Inside, provide ample space for each goat to rest and move around comfortably, with clean, dry bedding to lie on.

Like with other livestock, a balanced diet is critical to maintaining the health and productivity of goats. While goats are seen as animals that will eat anything, their nutritional needs are specific. A diet primarily composed of forage, such as grass, hay, or browse, should be supplemented with grain-based feed, especially for lactating nannies or growing kids. Essential minerals and salts should be made available through a lick or mixed into their feed to prevent deficiencies. Fresh, clean water, accessible at all times, is equally critical for their health.

Breeding goats brings the joy of kidding and the responsibility of ensuring the nannies' and their offspring's health and safety. As a responsible goat owner, you should understand the breeding cycle, recognize the signs of labor, and intervene if necessary. Goats typically have a gestation period of approximately 150 days, with the doe requiring increased nutritional support as she nears kidding. Signs that kidding is imminent include restlessness, vocalization, and a noticeable drop in her abdomen. A well-prepared kidding kit and a clean, warm, and secure area for the doe to give birth can help the process go smoothly.

A human member of the household should be on hand to observe the birth. Following kidding, ensure the newborn kids nurse promptly to receive vital colostrum and monitor for any signs of distress. Kids grow rapidly, requiring a diet to support their development as they transition from milk to solid food. Vaccinations and routine health checks help safeguard against common diseases, ensuring a healthy start to their lives.

In integrating goats into your homestead, you embrace their utility in providing milk, meat, land management, and the vibrancy they add to daily life. These intelligent and social animals require attention, care, and a bit of patience, especially when it comes to securing their enclosures. Yet, the rewards of their presence, from the joy of watching them explore their surroundings to the satisfaction of producing your dairy and meat, are immeasurable. With the proper preparation and knowledge, goats can become an invaluable part of your self-sufficient homestead.

BEEKEEPING FOR HONEY AND POLLINATION

The hum of bees busily at work is a sign of a healthy garden. These small but mighty workers play a pivotal role in the ecosystem, pollinating plants and producing honey, a natural sweetener and medicinal marvel. For aspiring beekeepers, there are a few foundational steps you can take to set you on the path to success.

Laying the Groundwork for Beekeeping

Establishing a beekeeping operation starts with gathering knowledge and resources. A solid understanding of bee behavior and the right equipment pave the way for a fruitful endeavor. Essential preparations include:

- Education: Read books, take online courses, and join local beekeeping associations to absorb as much information as possible. Knowledge of bee biology and behavior is crucial.
- Equipment: Essential gear includes a bee suit, gloves, a hive tool, and a smoker. These tools ensure your safety and facilitate hive management.
- Hive selection: Various hive types, such as Langstroth, Top-Bar, or Warre, offer different advantages. Your choice will depend on your management style and goals.
- Bees can be obtained via nucleus colonies, packages, or swarms. Each method has nuances, with nucleus colonies often providing a gentler introduction for beginners.

Diving into beekeeping requires an initial investment of time and resources, but yields reward far beyond honey alone.

Seasonal Care for Bees:

Attentive care throughout the seasons ensures the health and productivity of your bee colony. From spring inspections to winter preparations, each period demands specific actions:

- Spring: Inspect the hive for health, queen presence, and signs of disease or pests. It is also the ideal time to manage the space within the hive to prevent swarming.

- Summer: Regular checks continue, with an eye on honey stores and room for expansion. It is also the peak season for honey production and potential extraction.
- Fall: Prepare the hive for winter by ensuring adequate food stores and reducing the hive's entrance to protect against pests.
- Winter: While bees require less intervention during winter, occasional checks on food levels and hive weight, which indicate stores, are necessary; depending on your climate, insulation may be needed.

This cycle of care, attuned to the rhythms of the seasons, fosters a robust and resilient colony capable of pollinating your garden and producing honey.

Harvesting Honey and Beeswax

Harvesting is a delicate process that, when done respectfully, ensures the colony's health while providing you with honey and beeswax. The timing and method of harvest play a critical role.

The best time to harvest is in late summer or early fall. Leave enough honey in the hive to ensure your bees have enough stores for winter. Use a bee brush or smoker to gently encourage bees away from the frames you plan to harvest. A manual or electric extractor can spin the honey out of the comb.

After extraction, strain the honey through a mesh filter to remove wax or debris, then store it in clean jars. Beeswax, collected from the cappings cut from the honeycomb or old combs, can be melted and filtered for use in candles, balms, and more.

When done correctly, this process is rewarding for the beekeeper and maintains the health of the bees, underscoring the symbiotic relationship at the heart of beekeeping.

The Far-reaching Impact of Bees on Homesteads

Bees are not just honey producers. They're also key players in the ecosystem, adept at pollinating various plants. This service is essential for producing fruits, vegetables, and seeds, enhancing the diversity and yield of your garden and beyond.

The benefits include increased fruit and vegetable yields, contributing to food security and variety on the homestead. Pollination is crucial for plant reproduction and diversity, so introducing bees improves the garden's health. They don't only pollinate the plants you've grown, either. Bees also pollinate wild plants, supporting the local ecosystem and improving ecological balance.

By nurturing bees, you enrich your homestead and sustain the intricate web of life that thrives in the surrounding environment.

With its blend of art and science, beekeeping is a practice that calls for patience, care, and a willingness to learn. You'll enjoy the sweet taste of honey and the vibrant bloom of your garden. You gain valuable produce and become a steward of these remarkable creatures whose work underpins the health and productivity of our ecosystems.

RABBITS AND PIGS: SMALL-SCALE SOLUTIONS

Rabbits and pigs are often overlooked in favor of more traditional livestock; they offer many benefits that can significantly enrich a self-sufficient lifestyle.

Raising Rabbits for Meat and Fiber

Rabbits hold a unique position on the homestead, capable of providing both high-quality meat and luxurious fiber. Their small stature and efficient breeding capabilities make them an excellent choice for those with limited space. Here are vital considerations for raising rabbits:

- Housing: Rabbits require a clean, dry, and well-ventilated environment. Hutch designs vary, but they must protect rabbits from the elements and predators. Wire flooring is standard and designed to keep the living area clean.
- Feeding: A diet of high-quality pellet feed supplemented with hay ensures proper nutrition. Fresh vegetables are introduced in moderation to prevent digestive issues.
- Care: Conduct regular health checks for signs of illness and proper grooming for fiber breeds. Angora rabbits, for instance, need frequent brushing to prevent the matting of their wool.
- Processing Meat and Harvesting Fiber: Learning humane processing methods is vital for raising rabbits for meat. For fiber rabbits, shearing or plucking during molting periods yields valuable material for spinning.

Pig Breeds for Small Homesteads

With their intelligence and versatility, pigs can be an asset to any homestead, turning scraps into high-quality meat and contributing to land management. When selecting pig breeds for small-scale operations, consider the following:

- Size and temperament: Smaller breeds, like the American Guinea Hog, occupy less space and are easier to handle. Their gentle nature makes them suitable for homesteads with children.

- Feeding: Pigs are omnivores and thrive on a varied diet. While kitchen scraps can supplement their diet, ensure they receive a balanced pig feed to meet their nutritional needs.
- Housing: Pigs require a sturdy pen to contain them and a shelter to protect them from weather extremes. They also need a wallow or mud pit to cool off in warmer months.
- Space requirements: Smaller pig breeds need ample space to roam and forage, allowing exercise and supporting well-being.

Integrating Rabbits and Pigs into the Homestead Cycle

Rabbits and pigs can play pivotal roles in achieving a closed-loop system on the homestead. Their contributions include:

- Waste management: Pigs can consume a wide range of food scraps, reducing waste and converting it into valuable manure. Both rabbit and pig manure are excellent additions to compost, enriching the soil for vegetable gardens and crop fields.
- Soil improvement: Pigs' natural behaviors, such as rooting, help aerate the soil and reduce weed populations, preparing land for planting.
- Pasture management: Moving pigs across different areas prevents overgrazing and soil compaction while naturally fertilizing the land. For rabbits, rotating outdoor runs or employing tractor pens allows for natural foraging while protecting the pasture.
- Fiber production: Rabbits, especially wool breeds, provide a renewable source of fiber for clothing and crafts, adding value to the homestead economy.

By embracing rabbits and pigs as part of your homestead, you tap into a wellspring of resources that bolster your independence. These animals prove that even small-scale operations can yield significant rewards, from the soft wool of rabbits to the cheerful grunts of pigs bringing life and vitality to the homestead. You ensure your animals' well-being and your homestead's health and productivity through thoughtful management and care.

MAKE A DIFFERENCE WITH YOUR REVIEW

UNLOCK THE POWER OF GENEROSITY

> "True happiness is found in helping others."
>
> — ANONYMOUS

People who give without expectation live longer, happier lives and make more money. So, if we've got a shot at that during our time together, let's try it.

To make that happen, I have a question for you...

Would you help someone you've never met, even if you never got credit for it?

Who is this person you ask? They are like you. Or, at least, like you used to be. Less experienced, wanting to make a difference, and needing help, but needing help figuring out where to look.

Our mission is to make off-grid homesteading accessible to everyone. Everything we do stems from that mission, and the only way for us to accomplish it is by reaching… everyone.

This is where you come in. Most people judge a book by its cover (and its reviews). So here's my ask on behalf of a struggling new homesteader you've never met:

Please help that hopeful homesteader by leaving this book a review.

Your gift costs no money and takes less than 60 seconds to make real, but it can change a fellow beginner's life forever. Your review could help…

...one more small business provides for their community.
...one more entrepreneur supports their family.
...one more person finds meaningful work.
...one more reader transforms their life.
...one more dream come true.

To get that 'feel good' feeling and help this person for real, all you have to do is...and it takes less than 60 seconds...

Leave a review.

Simply scan the QR code to leave your review:

If you feel good about helping a faceless beginner, you are my kind of person. Welcome to the club. You're one of us.

I'm even more excited to help you achieve self-sufficiency faster than you can imagine. You'll love the lessons and strategies we share in the coming chapters.

Thank you from the bottom of my heart. Now, back to our regularly scheduled programming.

Your biggest fan,

Wellness Wisdom Works

PS - Fun fact: If you provide something of value to another person, it makes you more valuable to them. If you'd like goodwill straight from another beginner - and believe this book will help them - send it their way.

7

ENERGY INDEPENDENCE

Energy is a necessity on a modern homestead. How much you need to generate depends on the property size and lifestyle. That's the first detail you'll need to figure out before researching wind turbines or solar panels.

Empower yourself by listing all your electrical appliances and devices to understand your energy consumption. Note how many watts each consumes and their daily use duration. This exercise isn't just an eye-opener about where your energy goes; it's a powerful tool that helps you size your solar power system to meet your needs.

Once you've determined each appliance's average daily wattage needs, add these numbers to your daily watt-hour total. From there, it's time to research your environment. If you plan to use solar panels, check with your local weather station to determine the average peak sunlight hours your location receives. You can gather similar information about wind speeds if you plan to install turbines. This knowledge will help you choose the best size and format for your renewable energy infrastructure, including energy storage solutions.

CONDUCTING AN ENERGY AUDIT

Renewable energy is cleaner than that derived from fossil fuels, but that doesn't mean you want to waste it. The research you'll do before installing solar, wind, or other renewable energy systems is the perfect opportunity to become more energy efficient overall. To start, thoroughly audit your homestead's energy use. This process involves a detailed examination of your energy consumption, identifying areas where you can reduce energy use and increase efficiency.

- Listing appliances and devices: Catalog all electrical appliances and devices, noting their energy ratings and usage patterns.
- Monitoring energy consumption: Use a power meter to track the energy use of individual appliances over a set period, highlighting energy hogs and efficiency stars.
- Inspecting insulation and seals: Check windows, doors, and insulation for leaks or drafts that could lead to unnecessary heating or cooling costs.
- Evaluating lighting: Account for all lighting fixtures, noting the types of bulbs and areas that may benefit from natural lighting solutions.

This audit clearly shows energy use, setting the stage for targeted improvements.

SOLAR POWER SYSTEMS

The sun isn't just a celestial body that marks the passage of days; it's an abundant energy source. Solar power technology has been refined over the years and is more accessible today than ever, which is a beacon of hope for off-grid living. Let's look at how to harness solar energy and maintain a solar power system for the long haul.

Components of a Solar Power System

Understanding the pieces that make up a solar power system demystifies its operation. Here's a breakdown, including the types of solar panels and wind turbines available:

- Solar panels are the workhorses, capturing sunlight and converting it into direct current (DC) electricity.
- Batteries are essential for storing energy when the sun isn't shining, especially for off-grid systems.
- Inverter: This device converts DC electricity from your panels (or batteries) into alternating current (AC), the electricity most household appliances use.
- Charge controller: It regulates the flow of electricity from the panels to the batteries, preventing overcharging and damage.

Installation Best Practices

Installing a solar power system involves more than mounting panels on your roof. Here are detailed steps to ensure a smooth setup, including the necessary tools and safety precautions:

1. Site assessment: Choose a location with clear, unobstructed access to sunlight. Roofs are standard, but ground-mounted systems work well if space allows.
2. Mounting the panels: Ensure the mounting system is securely anchored, considering your roof type and weight capacity. Proper angling towards the sun maximizes efficiency.
3. Wiring: Following electrical codes, connect the panels to the inverter and batteries, ensuring all connections are tight and protected from the elements.
4. Inspection and testing: Before the entire operation, have a professional inspect the installation and test the system to ensure everything functions as intended.

Routine Maintenance for Longevity

Like any significant investment, a solar power system requires care to maintain efficiency over the years. Solar panels are low-maintenance overall, but a few regular actions can prolong the system's life and performance. Let's delve into the importance of routine maintenance and the specific tasks involved:

- Panel cleaning: Dust, leaves, or snow can reduce panel efficiency. To keep them operating optimally, gently clean the panels a few times a year or after significant storms.
- Battery care: For systems with batteries, regular checks on connections, fluid levels (for lead-acid batteries), and overall battery health are crucial.
- System monitoring: Monitoring energy production and consumption helps identify issues early. Many inverters come with monitoring software for easy tracking. In this section, we'll also discuss common problems that may arise and how to troubleshoot them.

- Professional check-ups: Having a professional inspect the system annually can catch potential issues before they escalate, ensuring your system remains in top condition.

Solar power systems offer a pathway to energy independence that aligns with sustainable living principles. By understanding your energy needs and adhering to the best installation and maintenance practices, you can fully use the sun's potential to power your homestead life. Let's also explore the environmental benefits of solar power, including reduced carbon emissions and conservation of natural resources.

WIND TURBINES FOR HOMESTEADS

While solar panels are the more accessible and popular choice for off-grid power, they're not the only way to generate your energy. On some properties, wind turbines are a more reliable energy source and can also be used in tandem with solar systems for a more resilient energy solution. However, it's essential to be aware of these systems' potential challenges and limitations, which we'll discuss in this section.

Evaluating Your Site for Wind Energy

There are several factors to consider when determining the feasibility of wind turbines, including:

- Average wind speed: An area's average wind speed, typically measured at 33 feet above the ground, dictates the amount of power a turbine can generate. Sites with average wind speeds of at least 9 miles per hour are suitable for wind energy projects.
- Obstructions: Trees, buildings, and natural land formations can significantly impact wind flow. An open,

unobstructed space allows for optimal wind turbine performance.

- Local climate: Regions prone to high winds or storms require turbines that can withstand such conditions without sustaining damage.
- Legal and environmental constraints: Ensure compliance with local zoning laws and consider the potential impact on local wildlife and ecosystems.

Performing a wind site assessment with the help of a professional sets the groundwork for a successful wind energy project.

Choosing the Right Wind Turbine

Selecting a wind turbine that matches your energy needs and environmental conditions is critical. Wind turbines come in two main designs:

- Horizontal Axis Wind Turbines (HAWTs): Traditional windmill-style turbines are ideal for areas with consistent wind directions; they typically require more space and a higher initial investment but offer greater efficiency.
- Vertical Axis Wind Turbines (VAWTs): Their design allows them to capture wind from any direction, making them well-suited for areas with variable wind patterns. They are also often more compact, making them a good choice for residential properties with limited space.

When choosing a wind turbine, consider:

- Power output: Match the turbine's power output to your energy needs and your site's average wind speed.
- Noise: Some turbines produce more noise than others.

Consider the proximity to living spaces and the potential impact on neighbors.
- Maintenance requirements: Understand your chosen turbine model's maintenance and upkeep needs.

A thoughtfully chosen wind turbine maximizes energy production and integrates seamlessly into your homestead's landscape and lifestyle.

Installation Considerations

Setting up a wind turbine requires more than just putting up a tower and attaching blades; it involves addressing several logistical and technical considerations.

- Tower height: Taller towers reach stronger winds but require more robust foundations and clearances. The key is to balance height with practicality and local regulations.
- Location: The turbine's placement is critical. Choose a placement with minimal obstructions, stable ground, and easy access for maintenance.
- Foundation: Depending on the turbine size and soil type, different foundation options, from simple concrete pads to more complex designs, may be required.
- Electrical infrastructure: Plan the connection between the turbine and your home or battery storage, ensuring safe and efficient energy transmission.

Careful planning on the above points ensures that your wind turbine will be a reliable and efficient power source for years.

Maintenance and Safety:

Ongoing maintenance and adherence to safety protocols are crucial for the longevity and performance of your wind turbine. They include the following:

- Blade inspection and cleaning: Inspect blades for damage and clean them to maintain aerodynamic efficiency.
- Lubrication: Regularly lubricate moving parts to reduce wear and prevent failures.
- Electrical system checks: Monitor the electrical system for signs of wear or damage, ensuring connections remain secure and corrosion-free.
- Storm preparations: In areas prone to severe weather, have a plan for securing or lowering the turbine to prevent damage.

Safety is paramount. Always follow manufacturer guidelines for maintenance and repairs, and consider professional assistance for tasks that require climbing the tower or handling electrical components.

BIOFUEL OPTIONS FOR HEATING AND COOKING

Many discussions of alternative energy focus on sources that produce electricity. These are undoubtedly necessary for a self-sufficient lifestyle but aren't the only fuel you may need on your homestead. Biofuels are a renewable and locally producible solution for heating and cooking needs. There's an array of promising biofuels for homesteads, each utilizing its production methods and may require unique adaptations to appliances you plan to fuel with them. Let's dig deeper into each and the advantages and hurdles associated with their use.

Types of Biofuels Suitable for Homesteads

Biofuels, derived from organic materials, present a versatile range of options for the homesteader. Each category caters to different energy needs and requires different resources for their production. Key types include:

- Biodiesel, a cleaner-burning replacement for traditional diesel, is created from vegetable oils or animal fats. Its use in diesel engines, from tractors to generators, makes it valuable.
- Ethanol, a potent fuel often blended with gasoline to power various engines and stoves, is fermented from crops such as corn or sugarcane.
- Biogas, comprising methane and carbon dioxide, is produced through the anaerobic digestion of organic waste. It offers a solution for energy production and waste management.

Producing Biofuels on Your Homestead

For those inclined towards DIY projects, producing biofuels at a small scale is achievable with some dedication and ingenuity. The primary production methods for each category are as follows:

- Biodiesel production: Requires processing equipment to convert used cooking oil or animal fats into fuel through a chemical reaction known as transesterification.
- Ethanol fermentation: Involves fermenting sugar or starch-rich materials into alcohol and then distilling the mixture to increase the ethanol concentration.
- Biogas digesters: Small-scale digesters can convert kitchen scraps, animal manure, and plant waste into biogas. They

require airtight containers to collect and store the produced gas.

While each process demands specific knowledge and equipment, the ability to turn waste materials into energy resources is well worth the upfront time and money investment for many homesteaders.

Biofuel-powered Appliances

Certain appliances can be purchased or modified to utilize these alternative energy sources to make the most of biofuels. Exam to make the most of biofuels:

- Biodiesel generators and tractors: Many diesel engines can run on biodiesel with minimal modifications, offering a sustainable option for powering machinery and equipment.
- Ethanol stoves: Specialized stoves designed for ethanol offer a clean-burning solution for cooking, though they may require adaptations for safe fuel storage and handling.
- Biogas cookers and heaters: Appliances adapted for biogas use can transform kitchen and heating solutions on the homestead, tapping into the continuous supply of gas from a biodigester.

These adaptations reduce reliance on conventional fuels and demonstrate biofuels' versatility and practicality in everyday homestead life.

Benefits and Challenges of Biofuels

The integration of biofuels into homesteading practices brings a spectrum of environmental and economic benefits, such as:

- Renewability: Biofuels offer a sustainable energy option, reducing dependency on fossil fuels and contributing to a lower carbon footprint.
- Waste reduction: Biofuels promote a closed-loop system by utilizing waste products for energy, enhancing the sustainability of homestead operations.
- Energy independence: Producing biofuels empowers homesteaders with greater energy autonomy, lessening the impact of fluctuating fuel prices.

However, potential obstacles and challenges must also be acknowledged, including:

- Resource allocation: The production of biofuels, especially ethanol, can require significant amounts of feedstock, which might compete with food production or land use.
- Technical complexity: Some biofuel production methods involve complex processes and equipment, posing a steep learning curve for beginners.
- Regulatory hurdles: Local regulations may govern the production and use of biofuels, necessitating careful navigation to ensure compliance.

Navigating these pros and cons requires a thoughtful approach. You must weigh the immediate and long-term impacts on the homestead and the broader environment. Carefully consider which biofuels best align with your resources and needs.

ENERGY STORAGE SOLUTIONS

Energy storage enables you to capture the warmth and sunlight of summer and release them to counter winter's chill and gray skies. Several battery technologies exist, and the most suitable one for your homestead will depend on your specific energy storage requirements and the ease of integration into your energy system.

Understanding Energy Storage Needs

If you're preparing a meal, you don't go to the store first and buy tons of each ingredient–you check the recipe first to see how much you'll need. The same concept applies to your homestead's energy. Before you start pricing batteries and storage systems, take the time to understand your storage requirements. Begin by looking at your energy consumption patterns and production capabilities; by tracking how much energy you consume daily and comparing it with the amount generated by your solar panels or wind turbine, you identify the storage capacity needed to bridge gaps, especially during low production or peak consumption.

To start, track your daily energy usage and generation over several months. Make sure you note seasonal variations on both sides of this equation. Pay special attention to periods of underproduction or excess consumption, which indicate a need for more storage. Consider future changes if you plan to add more appliances or expand your homestead, which could increase energy demands.

You can best tailor your storage system through meticulous observation and calculation for today's needs and the evolving demands of your off-grid life.

Battery Types and Technologies

The heart of any energy storage solution is the battery, a technology that has seen significant advancements in recent years. Three main types have emerged as frontrunners for off-grid applications, each with its distinct characteristics:

- Lead-acid batteries: A time-tested solution, these batteries are known for their reliability and lower upfront cost. However, they require regular maintenance, including water top-ups, and have a shorter lifespan than other types.
- Lithium-ion batteries: Lithium-ion batteries offer a longer lifespan, have a higher energy density, and require minimal maintenance. Their efficiency and compact size make them desirable, albeit with a higher initial investment.
- Flow batteries: A newer entrant to the field, flow batteries excel in long-duration energy storage. They offer scalability and have no degradation over time, making them ideal for extensive off-grid systems. However, their complexity and cost may pose barriers for smaller applications.

No one type of battery is perfect for every application. Instead, consider your specific energy needs, budget constraints, and maintenance capacity, using these factors to guide you to the energy storage solution that best meets your homestead's needs.

System Integration and Management

Once you've chosen the right battery style, it's time to actively integrate it into your system. The steps will vary based on the energy you're harvesting, your selected battery model, and the wiring and other components your system employs. If you need more experience in electrical work or energy storage, seek guidance from a professional.

Linking your batteries to solar panels or wind turbines requires careful wiring. Charge controllers will be required to manage the flow of electricity. You'll also need an inverter to convert stored DC power into usable AC power for your home. Different inverters have different energy capacities, so you want to ensure your inverter can handle the input from your storage system.

Modern battery systems often include software for monitoring energy flow and battery health. These tools can be very beneficial, enabling informed energy and storage management decisions. If your battery doesn't include these features, you can buy stand-alone devices to accomplish the same thing.

Maintenance and Safety of Storage Systems

The longevity and safety of your energy storage system rest on a foundation of regular maintenance and adherence to safety protocols. For each type of battery, specific practices ensure optimal performance and prevent accidents:

- Visual inspections: Regularly check for signs of wear, corrosion, or leakage, particularly in lead-acid batteries.
- Temperature control: Keep batteries in a temperature-controlled environment to prevent overheating or freezing, which can damage cells and reduce efficiency.
- Ventilation: Lead-acid and flow batteries emit gasses during charging and discharging, which require well-ventilated areas to dissipate safely.
- Regular testing: Perform capacity tests to gauge battery health and identify when replacements are needed.

Safety is paramount. Always follow manufacturer guidelines and wear appropriate protective gear when handling batteries. Study some first aid measures and have emergency contacts readily available during spills or exposure to battery materials.

REDUCING ENERGY CONSUMPTION

The adage "less is more" rings especially true in the quest for a self-reliant lifestyle. Lower energy consumption means less power you need to generate and store, making it sustainably easier to develop your energy on-site. Let's consider some practical steps to minimize energy usage on your homestead, from auditing your consumption to adopting energy-saving behaviors.

Energy-efficient Appliances and Lighting

The excellent news is that homesteaders aren't the only people interested in saving energy in the modern world. The rise in eco-consciousness across the board has spurred the development of many energy-efficient appliances and lighting options. Some straightforward avenues to reducing energy consumption include:

- Energy Star-rated appliances: Look for appliances with the Energy Star label, which indicates they meet or exceed the energy efficiency guidelines set by the Environmental Protection Agency (EPA).
- LED bulbs: Replace incandescent and halogen bulbs with LED alternatives that consume up to 90% less power and last significantly longer, reducing both energy use and replacement costs.
- Smart thermostats: Install a smart thermostat that learns your heating and cooling preferences and adjusts for optimal energy use throughout the day.

While seemingly simple, these swaps can lead to substantial reductions in energy consumption without sacrificing comfort or convenience.

Passive Design Strategies

The design and orientation of your homestead significantly impact its energy consumption, especially concerning heating, cooling, and lighting. Passive design strategies harness natural environmental conditions to maintain comfortable temperatures and lighting levels:

- Maximizing natural light: Position windows and skylights to capture daylight, reducing the need for artificial lighting.
- Thermal mass materials: Incorporate stone or concrete that can absorb and slowly release heat, stabilizing indoor temperatures.
- Strategic shading: Use landscaping, awnings, and trellises to shade windows during the hottest parts of the day, minimizing the need for air conditioning.
- Cross-ventilation: Design windows and doors to facilitate cross-ventilation, drawing cool air in and pushing hot air out, naturally reducing cooling needs.

Implementing these strategies during construction or renovation can significantly lower energy demands, enhancing your homestead's sustainability and comfort.

Behavioral Changes for Energy Saving

Ultimately, the most sophisticated systems and strategies can only go so far without mindful usage patterns. Minor behavioral adjustments can profoundly impact reducing energy consumption, such as:

- Unplugging devices: Disconnect chargers and appliances when not in use to prevent "vampire" energy loss.
- Adjusting thermostat settings: To reduce heating and cooling loads, set your thermostat slightly lower in winter and higher in summer.
- Using appliances wisely: To maximize efficiency, run dishwashers and washing machines with full loads and during off-peak hours.
- Conserving water: Shorten showers and fix leaks promptly to reduce hot water use, one of the more significant energy consumers in many homes.

These habits, cultivated over time, contribute to a culture of conservation that complements technological and design-based efficiency measures.

The pursuit of efficiency is an ongoing journey, not a final goal. Thoughtful actions such as conducting energy audits, employing passive design strategies, and making daily behavioral changes are milestones along this path. All these steps aim to minimize our environmental impact while fulfilling our needs. When living sustainably is your goal, every action—big or small—helps create a harmonious relationship with the natural world.

8

WATER WISDOM

CRAFTING YOUR HOMESTEAD'S LIFELINE

Water is a source of growth refreshment when harnessed with respect. Yet, for those living off the grid, acquiring it is more complex than turning on a tap. Instead, it's necessary to understand water cycles and use innovative approaches to draw, purify, and conserve this precious resource, ensuring every drop counts towards nurturing your homestead.

SOURCING WATER OFF-GRID

Discovering water off-grid is a journey that combines traditional wisdom and modern ingenuity. Here are a few paths you might explore, empowering you to take control of your water source:

- Wells: Drilling a well and directly tapping underground aquifers are standard solutions. The depth, type, and cost can vary widely, so it's wise to consult with neighbors or a local expert to learn more about water availability in your area.

- Springs: Capturing water from a natural spring combines reliability with purity. Bringing the water to your home often requires a collection box and a gravity-fed system.
- Rainwater collection involves installing gutters on your roof to catch rainwater, which is then directed into storage tanks. With the proper filtration, this can be an excellent source of clean water. The collected rainwater can be used for various purposes, including irrigation, laundry, and drinking water with the proper purification.

Each source offers benefits and drawbacks, and determining the best choice for a homestead depends on geography, climate, and legal factors. Opting for a mixed approach typically yields optimal results, maintaining a consistent supply of fresh water while preserving the natural balance of your land.

Purification and Filtration

Even if it looks clear and clean, natural water is often unsafe for humans to drink straight from its source. It can contain various contaminants, including bacteria, viruses, parasites, chemicals, and heavy metals. Before it can be considered potable, it must be filtered using approaches such as:

- Boiling: The most straightforward method, effective against pathogens but energy-intensive for large quantities.
- Ceramic filters can remove bacteria and protozoa from rainwater or spring water. Regular cleaning extends their lifespan.

- Reverse osmosis systems: These systems can remove many contaminants for a thorough solution, though they require a significant initial investment and maintenance.

To choose the suitable method, consider the initial quality of your water and your financial and energy resources. In many cases, combining methods can give you efficiency and peace of mind that your water is pure and safe to consume.

Water System Infrastructure

The infrastructure of your water system will determine how water moves from its source to your tap and involves these components:

- Pumps: A pump becomes necessary if gravity can't do the job. Solar-powered pumps offer an off-grid solution, reducing the need for external power sources.
- Gutters and downspouts: Gutters, Installed along the edges of roofs, catch rainwater and direct it into downspouts, which channel the water to storage tanks.
- Pipes: Piping water from its source to your home and throughout requires planning. Insulation might be necessary to prevent freezing in colder climates.
- Storage tanks: Storage tanks are crucial for collecting rainwater or pumping water from a well. They must be sized according to usage and protected from contamination and freezing.

A well-planned infrastructure minimizes waste and ensures water is available when and where you need it, with the least energy expenditure.

Conserving Water

On an off-grid homestead, every drop of water is a precious resource. By implementing these water conservation strategies, you can actively contribute to the sustainability of your homestead:

- Efficient fixtures: Low-flow faucets, showers, and dual-flush toilets reduce water usage indoors without sacrificing functionality. Keep the fixtures and pipes well-maintained to avoid leakage waste from leaks.
- Mulching: A thick layer of mulch in garden beds retains moisture, reduces evaporation, and minimizes the need for watering.
- Drip irrigation: Delivers water directly to the root zone of plants, minimizing waste and reducing evaporation compared to traditional sprinkler systems.
- Mindful water usage: Practices such as turning off the tap when brushing teeth, capturing tap water while waiting for it to warm up and using it to water plants, or reusing cooking water instill a culture of conservation.

GREYWATER SYSTEMS AND USES

Greywater, relatively clean wastewater from baths, sinks, and washing machines, can be safely reused in your off-grid homestead. While it's considered waste in a traditional home, in your homestead, it's a valuable resource that can benefit your garden plants and soil, giving you confidence in its safety and usability.

Greywater differs from both fresh water and sewage in its composition. It's tainted but can be reused for specific non-potable purposes. This water typically contains traces of food, grease, hair, and certain household cleaning products, which, while not suitable for direct consumption, can still benefit garden plants and soil.

Designing a Greywater System

The layout of a greywater system on your homestead requires a thoughtful approach, ensuring it aligns with legal standards and health guidelines. The process begins with identifying the grey-water sources in your home, such as showers or washing machines. The next step is to direct this water away from the sewage system and towards your garden or landscaping. Simple systems might employ mulch basins or direct hose connections, while more complex setups could use filters and pumps to distribute water more widely. It's essential to consider the slope of your land, the distance from the source to the garden, and the type of plants you have when designing your system.

Before you start designing a greywater system, it's important to check local regulations. Some areas have specific requirements or restrictions on greywater use. Once you've determined the legal limits, consider the layout of your land. Using gravity to your advantage can minimize the need for mechanical pumping. During the system installation, ensure all greywater pipes are marked, preventing accidental contamination of freshwater supplies and keeping you, your family, and your animals safe and healthy. At the same time, you maximize your use of the water resources on your property.

Greywater Treatment Options

Greywater has significantly fewer impurities than sewage, but it still usually requires some treatment to make it suitable for reuse. Several low-tech, sustainable options exist, including:

- Biological filters: Use sand, gravel, or even specific plants like cattails, reeds, and papyrus to filter out solids and impurities naturally.
- Constructed wetlands: These systems mimic natural wetlands, providing excellent filtration by interacting with plants, microorganisms, and natural biochemical processes.
- Mulch filtration: Employ mulch pits or trenches where greywater can percolate through organic material, trapping solids and undergoing natural purification before reaching plant roots.

You can adapt these methods to suit the size of your homesteading activities, whether you have a small garden or extensive agricultural projects.

Best Practices for Greywater Use

Follow some recommended best practices to ensure the safe and effective use of greywater. These include avoiding using greywater on edible plants, using greywater for outdoor irrigation only, and ensuring that the greywater system is adequately maintained and regularly inspected.

Avoid storing greywater, as it can quickly develop harmful bacteria. Use it promptly within 24 hours.

- Be mindful of the products you use for laundry, dishwashing, and bathing. Biodegradable, phosphate-free soaps and detergents will minimize the risk of soil and plant damage.
- Distribute greywater under the soil surface or through drip irrigation systems to avoid contact with plant leaves and reduce the risk of pathogen transmission.

- Rotate greywater discharge areas to prevent soil saturation and the buildup of salts or chemicals from cleaning products.

When selecting plants for greywater irrigation, opt for those that are hardy and not intended for raw consumption. Ornamental plants, fruit trees, and certain hardy vegetables can thrive on greywater, provided they are not overly sensitive to the soap and nutrient levels.

Greywater usage contributes to sustainability by conserving fresh water and enriching the soil with a constant supply of moisture and organic matter. Practicing this embodies the principle that all resources are valuable, turning previous waste into a source of growth and resilience.

NATURAL CLEANING PRODUCTS AND METHODS

Every choice you make when you live off the grid impacts the land and your health. Natural cleaning products are a practical choice for homesteaders. After all, you won't need to filter chemicals from your greywater if they're never there in the first place. Conventional commercial cleaning products contain a lot of things you wouldn't want to ingest (and wouldn't want your plants or animals taken in either). Shifting to cleaning products crafted from simple, natural ingredients protects the environment and creates a safer, healthier living space.

Switching to natural cleaning products brings a host of benefits, both environmental and personal. These products reduce the influx of harmful chemicals into our water systems, supporting the delicate balance of local ecosystems. They also offer a safe alternative for families, especially those with young children or pets, minimizing exposure to irritants and toxic substances commonly found in traditional cleaners.

Crafting Your Cleaners

Creating homemade cleaning solutions is an art and a science. It doesn't just reduce your exposure to chemicals, either. It also allows you to customize them to meet your specific needs. Here are a few staples:

- All-purpose cleaner: Combine white vinegar, water, and lemon peel for a versatile cleaner suitable for most surfaces.
- Glass cleaner: Mix rubbing alcohol, vinegar, and water for a streak-free shine on windows and mirrors.
- Scrubbing paste: Baking soda mixed with water creates a gentle yet effective paste for tackling tough grime.

These recipes are a good starting point. You can experiment with adding other natural ingredients to alter their scent or adjust their cleaning power until you find the perfect blend for your homestead.

Harnessing the Power of Microorganisms

Using beneficial microorganisms for cleaning works with nature rather than against it. Effective Microorganisms (EM) technology, which employs a mix of beneficial bacteria and yeast, offers a way to clean and deodorize without harsh chemicals. These microorganisms break down organic matter, including dirt and grime, into harmless substances. Incorporating EM into your cleaning regimen promotes a healthier home environment and enhances soil and water health when used in greywater systems or compost.

9

FOSTERING A COMMUNITY ECONOMY:

BEYOND CASH

In an era where digital transactions flash across the globe in milliseconds, the ancient practice of bartering, a system where goods and services are exchanged without money, offers a refreshing testament to the power of community and direct exchange. Off-grid homesteaders can leverage bartering to reduce their reliance on cash and enrich their lives and those around them.

Bartering, a practice beyond simple item exchange, can be a game-changer for new homesteaders. It's a versatile concept that reduces living expenses and fosters invaluable community relationships. Bartering is a lifeline for those with limited cash flow but possessing skills or produce of great value.

By engaging in the swap, you tap into a network of shared resources, where the actual currency is the trust and rapport built among neighbors. In addition to cutting costs and laying the foundation for solid community relationships, bartering optimizes resource use. Surplus goods find a purpose, and services meet an immediate need without wastefulness. The many benefits of bartering make it a precious tool for homesteaders. It fosters community and mutual support, making each participant feel connected and valued.

Items and Services Ideal for Barter

The diversity of goods and services that can be bartered is as vast as the needs and creativity of the community. Here are some sought-after items and services in a homesteading context:

- Fresh produce: Vegetables, fruits, and eggs you've grown or raised can be highly desirable to those without the space or means to produce their own.
- Handmade crafts: From knitted blankets to carved wooden utensils, handmade items carry a personal touch that many cherish.
- Skills exchange: Offering expertise in areas like carpentry, plumbing, or gardening in exchange for another's skills can lead to mutually beneficial arrangements.
- Labor: Sometimes, offering to help with a big project, like barn raising or harvesting, is the most valuable commodity you can offer.

Negotiating Fair Trades

The art of negotiation in bartering is crucial. The aim is to create a fair exchange for all parties involved. Start with an open discussion about needs and offerings, setting the stage for a transparent and honest exchange. Assess the relative value of goods and services and strive for mutual agreement to avoid future conflicts.

When discussing the terms of the exchange, be flexible and open to counter offers. Sometimes, some discussion can lead to a creative solution. Once you've ironed out the terms, it's essential to document the agreement, especially for larger trades. In writing, detail what each party expects to give and receive and when to help avoid conflicts and maintain the strong community ties that bartering promotes.

Legal Considerations in Bartering

While bartering may seem like a straightforward person-to-person exchange, considering the legal aspects, especially regarding taxes, is essential. In some jurisdictions, the value of goods and services exchanged through bartering is taxable. Keeping records of significant trades can help you report accurately, making a written agreement even more beneficial.

Bartering, with its roots deep in human history, offers more than just an alternative to cash transactions; it fosters cooperation and mutual support. By engaging in this practice, homesteaders optimize their resources and create a network of shared prosperity that benefits everyone involved.

In embracing bartering, remember that the most successful trades are those where both parties feel they have gained something of value, not just in terms of the goods or services exchanged but also the satisfaction of contributing to a collective resilience. Through thoughtful negotiation and a spirit of generosity, bartering can become a cornerstone of your homestead's economy, enriching your life in ways far beyond the material. This sense of empowerment and purpose is a significant emotional benefit of bartering.

SELLING SURPLUS: FROM FARMERS MARKETS TO ONLINE

Transforming your homestead's bounty into a source of income validates your hard work and connects your products with those who seek authentic, home-grown quality. There are many avenues for selling surplus, from bustling farmers markets to the vast digital marketplace, offering strategies to enhance your presence and profitability. This connection with customers and their appreciation for your products can be a source of great satisfaction and recognition for homesteaders.

Identifying Marketable Surplus

Before you can sell, the first step is to discern which of your homestead's offerings are ripe for the market. It requires a keen eye for quality and an understanding of what sells. Popular categories to sell include:

- Seasonal produce: Highly sought after for their freshness and flavor, items like heirloom tomatoes, berries, or specialty greens catch buyers' attention.
- Preserved goods: Jams, pickles, and sauces extend the life of your harvest and appeal to customers yearning for homemade taste.
- Homestead crafts: Whether it's beeswax candles, knitted scarves, or handcrafted soaps, your unique creations can find a special place in the market.
- Fresh eggs and honey: Always in demand, these staples offer a steady income stream and draw in health-conscious consumers.

Navigating Farmers Markets

Farmers markets provide a vibrant venue for selling your goods directly to consumers while being part of a community of fellow growers and artisans.

Do some research before you sign up for a booth. Each market has its own set of rules and fees. Understanding these in advance ensures a smooth entry. Also, know the local regulations regarding the sale of homegrown or homemade products and what kind of licensing, insurance, or other legal things you should obtain before your first market day.

The next step is to design your booth. You can think of your market stall as your storefront. Make it inviting with clear signage and attractive displays. Offering samples can bring more browsers to your tent.

Another thing that will attract buyers is competitive yet fair pricing. When setting your prices, consider the cost of production and market rates. Making a personal connection sells even more than having the lowest price. Be ready to share stories about your homestead, offer advice on using your products, and learn from customer feedback.

Leveraging Online Platforms

The digital realm offers a boundless marketplace for your surplus, reaching customers beyond local boundaries. Here's how to navigate this space:

- Choose the right platform: Sites like Etsy excel for crafts, while eBay can be ideal for a broader range of goods. Niche online farmers markets are also emerging as popular spots for fresh produce and homestead products.
- Photography and descriptions: High-quality images and detailed, engaging product descriptions can significantly boost your online sales and help potential buyers understand their purchase.
- Shipping and handling: Offer clear information on shipping processes, costs, and packaging methods to ensure products arrive in perfect condition.
- Customer service: Prompt responses to queries and a friendly, helpful attitude build customer trust and encourage repeat business.

Building a Brand for Your Homestead

A strong, cohesive brand sets your homestead's products apart in a crowded market, fostering recognition and loyalty. It starts with the visual details of your store and products. Choose a name, logo, and color scheme that reflects the essence of your homestead and its values. Once you've established the brand, keep it consistent across all platforms and packaging to reinforce it in customers' minds.

Your homestead has a unique story. Share it through product descriptions, social media posts, and customer interactions. Stories of sustainable practices, heirloom varieties, or traditional crafting techniques resonate with consumers. You can use that story to build a following through regular, engaging posts on platforms like Instagram or Facebook. Share behind-the-scenes glimpses of your homestead, celebrate harvests, and announce new products.

Consider other ways to connect with customers besides a solid social media presence. For example, you can start an email newsletter to inform your most loyal customers about your homestead's goings-on. The newsletter's content can include exclusive offers, upcoming market appearances, and new product launches.

With these strategies, selling your homestead's surplus transforms a mere transaction into an opportunity for connection and community building. Whether through the vibrant atmosphere of a local farmers market or the global reach of online platforms, your products carry the essence of your homestead into homes and hearts, fostering a deeper appreciation for the labor of love that is homesteading.

HOMESTEAD FINANCIAL MANAGEMENT TOOLS

Managing the financial aspects of a homestead requires more than just a keen intuition for saving and spending. It's a meticulous process of planning, tracking, and analyzing that ensures the sustainable growth of your homestead. Using the right tools and methods can streamline this process, making financial management an integrated part of your homesteading routine rather than a daunting task.

Budgeting for Homestead Operations

Creating a budget for homestead operations is the first step toward financial clarity and control. This budget should encompass all your expected income and expenses, clearly showing your financial health. Here are some practical steps to craft a comprehensive budget:

- List all income sources: Sales from surplus produce, income from off-homestead jobs, and any other regular financial inflows.
- Detail your expenses: Break down your costs into animal feed, seeds and gardening supplies, utility bills, and maintenance costs.
- Use budgeting software: Several applications can help you categorize expenses and income, set budget targets, and track your performance over time.
- Review and adjust regularly: Reviewing your homestead budget empowers you to adjust your spending and savings plans based on actual performance and changing circumstances.

Tracking and Analyzing Income Streams

With multiple potential income streams on your homestead, keeping track of what brings in money and what doesn't is crucial. Key points to remember:

- Maintaining detailed records: Keep invoices, receipts, and notes of all transactions related to your homestead's income-generating activities.
- Using spreadsheets or financial software: Tools like Excel or dedicated financial tracking software can help you organize this information and make it easily accessible.
- Regular analysis: Periodically review your income streams to identify trends, profitability, and areas for improvement or expansion.
- Seasonal adjustments: Some income streams may be seasonal. Recognizing these patterns can help you plan for lean periods and maximize peak times.

Investing in Homestead Growth

Investing in your homestead's infrastructure, diversification, and expansion ensures its long-term viability and success. Here's how to approach these investments:

- Prioritize based on ROI: Consider the return on investment of projects that have the potential to increase efficiency, productivity, or income significantly.
- Research funding options: Grants, loans, and crowdfunding can provide the capital needed for more significant investments. Thorough research can help you find the most suitable and cost-effective financing options.

- Start small: Test new projects on a small scale before committing significant resources, which can help you gauge their potential success without risking too much.
- Plan for the long term: Some investments may take longer. Having a long-term perspective is crucial when planning infrastructure upgrades or diversification projects.

Planning for Taxes and Savings

A proactive approach to taxes and savings can prevent surprises and ensure you're setting aside enough to meet your future goals. How to manage these aspects effectively:

- Understand tax obligations: Familiarize yourself with the tax laws that apply to your homestead's operations. These include income tax, sales tax on products sold, and property tax considerations.
- Use tax planning software or consult a professional: Tools designed for tax planning can help you estimate your liabilities and plan accordingly. In more complex situations, an experienced advisor might be necessary.
- Automate savings: Setting up automatic transfers to a savings account can help you consistently save a portion of your homestead income for future needs, investments, or emergencies.
- Diversify savings: Consider different savings vehicles, such as high-yield savings accounts, certificates of deposit, or investment accounts, to maximize the growth of your saved funds.

Integrating these financial management tools and practices into your homesteading routine can create a stable operational foundation to ensure preparation for the ups and downs of homestead life and position you for future growth and expansion. Proper financial management is as much a part of successful homesteading as tending to your crops or caring for your livestock. With a solid approach to budgeting, tracking, investing, and saving, you set the stage for a thriving, sustainable homestead that can support your family and contribute to your community for years.

DIVERSIFYING HOMESTEAD INCOME STREAMS

Achieving financial stability on a modern homestead often requires a creative and open-minded approach to income generation. Exploring revenue channels beyond the traditional can bolster your financial resilience and enrich your homesteading experience. There are diverse avenues through which homesteaders can expand their income. To make the best choices for yourself, you should carefully consider the potential benefits and risks while finding the right balance between innovation and sustainability.

Exploring Diverse Income Opportunities

There are many opportunities for income on your homestead. The more channels you have for money, the more financially resilient you'll be. Consider the following avenues:

- Agritourism: Inviting visitors to experience the rhythms of homestead life, from farm tours to overnight stays, taps into the growing desire for authentic agricultural experiences. Consider hosting workshops or farm-to-table dinners.
- Online courses: Sharing your homesteading expertise through digital platforms caters to a global audience eager to learn. Your knowledge has value, whether it's organic

gardening, artisan cheese making, or sustainable building techniques.
- Renewable energy credits: For those who have invested in renewable energy systems, selling excess power back to the grid or engaging in renewable energy certificate markets offers a way to monetize your sustainable initiatives.

Each path presents unique opportunities to draw upon your existing resources and expertise to reach new markets and diversify your revenue.

Assessing Risks and Rewards

Every new venture has unique risks and rewards. This dynamic landscape requires careful navigation. To effectively evaluate these opportunities, consider the following steps:

- Market research: Understanding the demand for your proposed offering and potential competition makes a more successful venture.
- Cost-benefit analysis: Calculate the initial investment and ongoing expenses against the projected income. This analysis should include tangible and intangible costs, such as time commitment and impact on quality of life.
- Pilot projects: Before fully committing, test your idea on a smaller scale. This approach allows you to gauge interest, refine your offering, and identify any unforeseen challenges with minimal risk.

By thoughtfully assessing each opportunity, you can make informed decisions aligning with your financial goals and homesteading ethos.

Balancing Time and Resource Investment

The pursuit of new income streams, while exciting, requires a reasonable allocation of your most precious resources: time and energy. To maintain this balance:

- Prioritize: Only some opportunities will be suitable for your homestead. Focus on those that leverage your strengths and align with your long-term vision.
- Set boundaries: Protecting your time and well-being is crucial. Establish limits on how much time you dedicate to new ventures, ensuring they stay within essential homestead operations and personal time.
- Seek efficiency: Automation and delegation, where possible, can help manage the workload. Consider investing in tools or hiring help for specific tasks to free up your time for high-priority projects.

Wisely managing your time and energy lets you explore new income avenues while keeping them a positive and sustainable addition to your homesteading life.

Sustainable Growth Strategies

When diversifying income and pursuing growth focusing on sustainability, expanding to respect the limits of your land, resources, and personal well-being entails. Select ventures that align with your homesteading values and embody the principles of sustainability, community, and stewardship.

Just as important is staying adaptable and being willing to evolve as you go. Stay open to feedback and adjust your strategies for successes and setbacks. This flexibility is vital to long-term sustainability, helping you to better plan for the future. Consider how each new venture will fit into the bigger picture of your homestead. Planning for growth and potential scaling back ensures that your income streams can adapt to changing circumstances.

You can create a more financially resilient and fulfilling life by approaching diverse income opportunities with intention and care, securing your homestead's financial foundation, and enriching your connection to the community and the broader ecosystem.

LEGAL CONSIDERATIONS AND INSURANCE FOR SMALL HOMESTEADS

For those who have woven their lives into the fabric of the land, understanding the legal landscape is as vital as knowing the physical one. The laws that govern our actions and protect our assets are intricate. A solid grasp of these principles ensures the homesteader's survival and flourishing.

Navigating Zoning and Business Regulations

Local zoning laws and business regulations differ among municipalities and can significantly impact your homestead's operations. Researching local zoning laws is essential to understanding the permissible activities on your property, which could influence everything from the structures you construct to the animals you rear.

Similarly, comprehending business regulations is crucial, especially if your homestead is involved in commercial activities, including sales tax collection, obtaining business licenses, and adhering to health department regulations for food products. Stay informed about any changes in these laws. Establishing rapport with local authorities or affiliating with a regional farming association can provide timely updates and assistance.

Choosing the Right Insurance Coverage

Selecting appropriate insurance is akin to building a financial fence around your homestead: it's about protection and peace of mind.

Property Insurance safeguards your home and outbuildings against damage or loss, covering a range of perils from natural disasters to theft, which is must-have coverage for any homesteader, regardless of what activities you do there.

Liability Insurance is essential if your homestead welcomes visitors, such as for farm tours, classes, or agritourism ventures. This insurance protects you against claims for injury or property damage. While you may never need to make a claim, you'll be happy you have coverage if someone falls ill or sustains an injury while touring your property.

Product Insurance becomes relevant if you're selling goods, especially food products. It offers protection against claims of illness or harm from your products. Some markets may also require event insurance before participating, so check the regulations of any you plan to attend.

Protecting Intellectual Property

Innovation and creativity often lead to unique products, brands, or inventions; protecting these assets is crucial. Depending on what you produce, there are three types of intellectual property protection: copyrights, trademarks, and patents.

Copyrights are automatic for original works of authorship, including recipes, books, and artwork. While registration isn't necessary, it does provide legal benefits.

Trademarks protect symbols, names, and slogans used to identify your goods or services. Registration strengthens your legal rights and helps prevent others from using similar marks.

Patents may be applicable if you've invented a new product or process. Obtaining a patent grants you exclusive rights to your invention, a process that requires a detailed application.

Preparing for Legal Disputes

Even with careful planning, disputes can arise. Preparing for these starts with carefully documenting customer, vendor, or neighbor agreements. Written contracts can prevent misunderstandings and provide clarity.

If disputes do occur, seek mediation. This process involves a neutral third party and often leads to amicable solutions without litigation. In some instances, it may be necessary to consult with legal professionals. An attorney familiar with agricultural and business law can be invaluable for navigating complex issues.

While legal, financial, and insurance considerations are less tangible than the soil you till, they are integral to the homestead's overall health and productivity. They form the framework within which you operate, offering protection and guidance as you navigate the complexities of living closely with the land. This understanding secures our present endeavors and paves the way for future growth.

10

FOSTERING COMMUNITY CONNECTIONS:

STRENGTHENING BONDS ON THE HOMESTEAD

Successful homesteading is different from the solitary endeavor many imagine. Community connections offer mutual benefits, from shared knowledge to collaborative opportunities, enriching the homesteading experience. When neighbors exchange tips on pest control, share a bumper crop, or lend a hand during the harvest, the collective resilience of the community grows.

A supportive community can turn challenges into shared victories and become a vital source of emotional support, practical advice, and camaraderie. Here, we explore how to cultivate these connections, ensuring that your homestead and community flourish together.

Networking and Collaboration Opportunities

Local agricultural networks, cooperatives, and online forums dedicated to homesteading and farming are where you can connect with fellow homesteaders. This kind of networking can spark opportunities for joint ventures, such as co-ops for purchasing bulk supplies, shared equipment use, or collective marketing efforts for homestead products.

To start, look up local agricultural extension offices, farming associations, or online communities dedicated to homesteading and sustainable agriculture. Find community meetings, seasonal events, or other gatherings you can participate in. The more you contribute, the more connections you'll make.

Consider what you can offer to the community. For example, if you have surplus harvest or unique skills. Even something as simple as a well-organized tool lending library can be a great starting point for collaboration.

Hosting or participating in community events strengthens ties and fosters a sense of belonging. Consider organizing events that cater to your community's interests and needs, like seed swaps and plant sales, skill-sharing sessions, or potlucks to celebrate your harvests with a communal meal. These events serve as educational opportunities and gatherings that enrich the community's social fabric.

Navigating Conflicts and Competition

Disagreements and competition can arise in a community with shared goals and values. Approach these situations with transparency, respect, and a willingness to find common ground. Remember, the goal is not to "win" but to find solutions that benefit the community. Mediation by a neutral party can ensure that all voices are heard and valued.

STARTING A COMMUNITY GARDEN OR COOPERATIVE

Creating a community garden or forming a cooperative stands as a testament to the power of collective action. These initiatives bring fresh, local produce closer to the table and encourage mutual aid among participants.

The steps to start a community garden are as follows:

1. Identify a suitable location: The quest for land might lead you to vacant lots, unused portions of public parks, or even large backyards offered by community members. The key is finding a space accessible to all who wish to participate.
2. Engage the community: Involve potential gardeners and supporters from the beginning to gauge interest and gather ideas.
3. Secure permissions and funding: Depending on the location, you may need approval from local authorities or landowners. This stage also involves raising funds for initial expenses such as soil, seeds, and tools, which might come from donations, grants, or fundraising events.
4. Organize volunteers and resources: Assign roles based on individual skills and interests, from gardening to communication. Establish a system for managing resources, ensuring that tools and supplies are used efficiently and responsibly.
5. Distribution of produce: Decide collectively how the fruits of labor will be shared among participants or if the surplus will be donated to local food banks, fostering a spirit of generosity.

Benefits of Agricultural Cooperatives

Agricultural cooperatives offer a structured way for small producers to amplify their impact. They allow members to pool resources, share risks, and access markets that might otherwise be out of reach. The advantages include:

- Economies of scale: Cooperatives can negotiate better prices by combining orders for seeds, tools, and other supplies.
- Shared equipment and infrastructure: Members can access machinery and storage facilities that would be too expensive to procure individually.
- Market access: Cooperatives can market products under a familiar brand, reaching customers through farmers' markets, CSA programs, and wholesale channels to open new revenue streams.
- Knowledge and skill sharing: Regular meetings and workshops provide avenues for learning, from sustainable farming techniques to business management, enriching the community's expertise.

Structuring a Cooperative

The foundation of a successful cooperative lies in its structure, which must be designed to meet the needs of its members while ensuring sustainability and growth. Considerations include:

- Governance: Adopt a democratic process, giving all members a voice in critical decisions. Elect a board of directors to oversee operations and represent the cooperative's interests.
- Membership rules: Define clear criteria for membership, including any required contributions of time, money, or resources, and outline the rights and responsibilities of members.
- Financial management: Establish transparent practices for managing the cooperative's finances, including setting aside reserves for future investments and distributing profits among members.

Community-Supported Agriculture (CSA) Models

CSAs represent a bridge between producers and consumers, offering a direct line for fresh, seasonal produce while providing small farmers with a reliable source of income. Launching a CSA requires thoughtful planning in areas including:

- Member subscriptions: Determine your CSA's structure, including the subscription period's length and the size and variety of produce boxes. Set a price that reflects the value of the produce and the effort involved in growing it.
- Production planning: Plan your planting schedule to ensure a steady supply of diverse produce throughout the season. Consider growing a mix of staples and unique varieties to keep members engaged.
- Communication and distribution: Regularly communicate with members about what to expect in their boxes, including recipes and storage tips. Organize convenient pick-up locations or consider delivery options for added value.

While starting a community garden or cooperative is challenging, it offers rich rewards. These initiatives provide tangible benefits in the form of fresh produce and shared resources and foster a stronger sense of community and mutual support.

WORKSHOPS AND SHARING SKILLS

As you navigate life on your homestead, you'll naturally develop a reservoir of knowledge and expertise amassed through trials, successes, and reflection. Sharing this wisdom through workshops, online platforms, and mentorship programs not only enriches others but also galvanizes the spirit of communal learning and growth.

Identifying Teachable Skills

Every homesteader possesses unique skills honed through hands-on experience and thoughtful adaptation to their environment. Reflect on the areas where you have gained proficiency and consider what might interest others, such as organic gardening and sustainable building techniques, homemade cheese making, and natural dyeing.

Gauge interest by asking your community what skills they wish to learn and posting queries in local online forums. Finally, consider the practicality of teaching the skill and the resources, space, and time required for hands-on learning.

Organizing Educational Workshops

Once you've pinpointed the skills you're eager to share, the next step is crafting an educational experience that's both informative and engaging. Organizing a successful workshop involves several key components:

- Venue selection: Choose a space that accommodates the workshop's nature, whether it's the open expanse of your garden for a permaculture design course or the warmth of your kitchen for a bread-making class.
- Material preparation: Ensure you have all the necessary materials and tools for participants. Consider preparing take-home resources, such as instructional handouts or starter kits.
- Pricing structure: Determine a price that reflects the value of the workshop while remaining accessible—factor in materials, your time, and the exclusivity of the knowledge.

- Promotion: Utilize local community boards, social media, and word-of-mouth to spread the word about your workshop. Engaging visuals and testimonials from past workshops can significantly boost interest.

Online Education Platforms

Through courses and tutorials, digital platforms let you share homesteading knowledge with a global audience. Start by researching platforms that align with your teaching style and content. Options range from dedicated course sites like Udemy to broader platforms like YouTube.

Develop your curriculum, breaking down your knowledge into digestible modules or videos. Ensure each segment offers clear, actionable information and includes visual demonstrations whenever possible.

Once you've created the course, engage with your online community by responding to comments, asking for feedback, and encouraging discussion. This interaction fosters a dynamic learning environment and encourages continued participation.

Mentorship and Internships

Mentorship or internship programs can provide a hands-on, immersive learning experience for the homesteading-curious. In exchange for sharing your knowledge, you'll get additional hands and fresh perspectives to enhance your homestead.

Consider what structure works best for your homestead, whether it's a short-term internship focused on a specific project or a longer-term mentorship that covers a broader range of skills. Clearly outline expectations, responsibilities, and any compensation or exchange, such as lodging, meals, or a stipend. Transparency ensures both parties benefit from the experience.

At its best, the mentor-mentee relationship is based on open dialogue and mutual learning. To foster this kind of relationship, encourage questions and discussion, share mistakes as valuable lessons, and celebrate successes together.

Through the sharing of skills and knowledge, homesteaders contribute to the resilience and growth of their communities and reaffirm their commitment to a life of learning and adaptation. Teaching becomes a reciprocal exchange, where the dissemination of wisdom nurtures a collective quest for sustainability and self-sufficiency. As homesteaders open their gates, literally and figuratively, to students, interns, and online followers, they sow the seeds of empowerment and inspire a new generation to forge their paths in harmony with the land.

EDUCATING CHILDREN ON THE HOMESTEAD

Raising children on a homestead offers a unique opportunity to blend daily life with hands-on learning, where the rhythms of nature serve as both classroom and curriculum. In this environment, children learn responsibility, science, math, and humanities through practical, earth-centered activities, fostering a profound connection with the natural world and instilling values of sustainability and self-reliance from a young age.

Weaving Homesteading Into Education

Integrating homesteading activities into a child's education transforms abstract concepts into tangible experiences. Here's how to seamlessly blend learning with living:

- Seasonal cycles: Use the changing seasons to teach about the cycles of life. Children can learn about solstices, equinoxes, and weather patterns through observation and participation in seasonal homestead tasks.
- Math in the garden: Planting a garden becomes a lesson in geometry when laying out beds, calculating the area for planting, or spacing seeds. Harvest yields can teach weights, measures, and percentages.
- Science in the soil: Composting introduces children to microbiology and the chemistry of soil health. Testing soil pH or observing the decomposition process highlights scientific principles.
- History and heritage skills: Engaging in traditional crafts and preservation techniques connects children with historical practices and cultural heritage, offering lessons in history, anthropology, and art.

Inspiring Projects for Young Homesteaders

Engaging in projects that captivate a child's imagination can instill a love for learning and a sense of stewardship for the earth. Consider these ideas:

- Build a pollinator garden: Encourage children to research and select plants that attract bees, butterflies, and other pollinators. This project teaches about plant-animal interactions, the importance of pollinators, and basic landscaping skills.
- Weather station: Setting up a simple weather station where children can track rainfall, temperatures, and weather patterns fosters an interest in meteorology and climate science.

- Recycled art: Use materials found around the homestead to create art projects, teaching the value of recycling while exploring creativity and resourcefulness.
- Cooking from the garden: Involve children in harvesting ingredients and preparing meals, linking lessons in nutrition, plant biology, and culinary skills.

Fostering Responsibility Through Chores

Assigning age-appropriate chores helps with the homestead's day-to-day operations and instills a sense of responsibility and accomplishment in children. Here are ways to make chores educational and empowering:

- Animal care: Feeding chickens, collecting eggs, or grooming animals teaches children about animal biology, nutrition, and care ethics.
- Garden maintenance: Weeding, watering, and harvesting can be assigned based on the child's age and ability, offering practical lessons in plant science and food production.
- Resource management: Involving children in water conservation efforts or solar energy monitoring can instill an early awareness of environmental management and sustainability practices.

Broadening Horizons Through Community Involvement

Children participating in community agricultural events expose them to a broader range of educational experiences. It reinforces the sense of belonging to a larger community and takes on the following forms:

- Youth agricultural programs: Enroll children in 4-H clubs, scouts, or local farming workshops where they can learn new skills and meet peers with similar interests.
- Volunteering: Volunteer at community gardens, farmers' markets, or environmental clean-up days to teach children the value of service and the impact of collective action.
- Agricultural fairs and competitions: Participating in local fairs, whether entering a vegetable growing contest or displaying a craft project, provides goals to work towards and a platform to showcase their achievements.

Incorporating these elements into a child's upbringing offers a multifaceted education that prepares them for future challenges. Through hands-on learning, responsibility, and community involvement, children grow up with an ingrained respect for the earth, a robust work ethic, and an enduring sense of curiosity and wonder about the natural world.

UTILIZING ONLINE RESOURCES AND SOCIAL MEDIA

The internet is invaluable for homesteaders, offering information and opportunities to connect with a global community. The online world is rich with resources to enhance homesteading knowledge and skills, from forums with gardening tips to webinars on sustainable living.

Leveraging Online Learning Resources

The pursuit of knowledge is a constant on any homestead. The internet is a treasure trove of educational resources, such as:

- Educational websites: Platforms such as Modern Farmer and Mother Earth News provide articles, guides, and tutorials covering all aspects of homesteading, from animal care to zucchini cultivation.
- Forums: Websites like Homesteading Today offer spaces where you can ask questions, share experiences, and receive advice from fellow homesteaders.
- Webinars and online courses: Many agricultural extension services and private experts host webinars and courses, offering deep dives into specific topics such as permaculture design or organic pest control.

Exploring these resources can fill knowledge gaps, introduce new techniques, and inspire innovations, all from the comfort of your homestead.

Building an Online Community

Creating a space where experiences, challenges, and successes can be shared is about building an audience and fostering a sense of belonging. This can be achieved through various online platforms:

- Social media: Platforms like Instagram and Facebook are perfect for sharing snapshots of daily life, from sunrise over the fields to the harvest's bounty.
- Blogs: Starting a homestead blog can be a more in-depth way to share your journey, offering stories, advice, and lessons learned along the way.
- YouTube channels: Video content can be a powerful tool for sharing how-to guides, tours of your homestead, and even the occasional humorous mishap.

As you build your online presence, remember to engage with your followers by responding to comments, asking for their input, and thanking them for their support. This two-way communication strengthens your community and provides valuable feedback.

Marketing Your Homestead Online

The Internet offers many marketing opportunities for homesteaders looking to sell products or services. Effective online marketing can significantly expand your reach, allowing you to connect with customers beyond your local area through strategies like:

- Social media marketing: Utilize platforms where your target audience is most active to share enticing images of your products, special offers, and behind-the-scenes glimpses of your homesteading process.
- SEO: Optimize your website or blog content for search engines to improve your visibility.
- Content creation: Regularly updating your blog, social media, or YouTube channel with engaging and relevant content keeps your audience interested and encourages them to share your content with others.

By strategically marketing your homestead online, you can turn your passion into a viable income source, reaching customers who value the authenticity and quality of homestead-produced goods.

Online Security and Privacy

While the Internet is a powerful tool, it's essential to be mindful of security and privacy, especially when sharing personal and business information. Be cautious about how much personal information you share online. Consider creating separate business accounts on social media to keep your personal life private. You can also control who sees your posts and personal information by using the privacy settings on social media platforms. When shopping online, ensure that any website where you conduct transactions uses encryption (look for "https" in the URL).

By taking a few simple steps to protect your online presence, you can safely enjoy the benefits of sharing your journey with the world.

11

PLANNING FOR THE FUTURE:

THE CORNERSTONE OF RESILIENT HOMESTEADING

In off-grid homesteading, growth is not merely a measure of physical expansion but a testament to adaptability, resilience, and foresight. From adapting to a changing climate to planning strategically for the future, this chapter will outline strategies for growing and thriving while maintaining the delicate balance between progress and preservation.

UNDERSTANDING CLIMATE VULNERABILITIES

The shifting patterns of our world's weather pose unique challenges to the off-grid homesteader. However, you are empowering yourself to take control of the situation by first fortifying your homestead against climate change, which involves a clear-eyed assessment of your local area's vulnerabilities. These vulnerabilities can range from reduced water availability and soil degradation to loss of biodiversity and increased risk of natural disasters. It's critical to:

- Conduct a risk assessment: Identify potential climate-related threats specific to your region. If you're in a coastal area, sea-level rise and hurricanes are your primary concerns, while drought is a more pressing issue in the arid regions.
- Monitor changes: Monitor local weather patterns, noting any shifts in rainfall, temperature extremes, or the onset of new pests and diseases. This ongoing observation helps you make timely adjustments to your homesteading practices.
- Stay informed: Utilize resources from local agricultural extensions, climate science reports, and community knowledge to stay updated on predictions and recommendations for your area.

Adaptive Agriculture Practices: Your Key to Climate Resilience

- Drought-resistant crops: Seek varieties known for their resilience to water stress. Consider experimenting with native plants or evolved heirloom varieties to thrive in local conditions.
- Water-saving irrigation methods: Techniques such as drip irrigation, mulching, and rainwater harvesting can significantly reduce water usage while ensuring crops receive the moisture they need.
- Soil conservation techniques: Protecting and enhancing your soil through cover cropping, reduced tillage, and organic amendments helps maintain its health and ability to withstand extreme weather conditions.

Infrastructure Resilience

A resilient homestead stands firm in the face of nature's tests, from storms to droughts. Strengthening your homestead's infrastructure involves:

- Flood defenses: If your area is prone to flooding, consider elevating structures, creating swales and rain gardens to manage runoff, and planting vegetation that can absorb excess water.
- Fire-resistant materials: In fire-prone regions, protect your homestead by building with fire-resistant materials, clearing vegetation around structures, and maintaining firebreaks.
- Wind-proofing structures: Secure roofs, reinforce structures, and plant windbreaks to minimize damage from high winds. This might include strategically planting trees and shrubs to shield your homestead from prevailing winds.

Community-led Adaptation Initiatives: Harnessing the Power of Collective Resilience

- Resource sharing: Pool resources with neighbors for shared water storage solutions, seed exchanges, or cooperative purchasing of resilient plant varieties to reduce costs and increase diversity.
- Knowledge exchange: Host community meetings or workshops to share strategies and experiences adapting to climate change. This can foster innovation and spread effective techniques more widely.

- Collaborative projects: Work together on larger projects that benefit the community, such as restoring local waterways, creating gardens with drought-resistant plants, or organizing fire preparedness drills.

By embracing these strategies, we shield our homesteads from the immediate impacts of climate change and contribute to the community's resilience.

EXPANDING AND SCALING UP

When considering an expansion, the first step is a thoughtful assessment of your current situation. This involves an honest appraisal of resources, market demand, and your capacity to manage increased responsibilities. Key considerations include:

- Resource inventory: Assess the availability of land, water, and other critical resources. Determine if your current infrastructure can support expansion or if additional investments are required.
- Market analysis: Understand the demand for your products or services. Conduct market research to identify trends, potential customers, and competition. This will help you gauge the viability of scaling up operations.
- Personal capacity: Reflecting on your capacity is crucial as you consider expanding. Your well-being and quality of life are essential, and expanding should not come at the expense of these. Consider whether expanding will impact your quality of life or if you'll need to hire extra help to manage the increased workload. Your capacity is a valuable resource that should be considered in your expansion plans.

Sustainable Scaling Practices

As you plan for expansion, integrating sustainable practices ensures that growth does not come at the expense of ecological or economic stability. Key practices include:

- Eco-friendly techniques: Adopt methods that minimize environmental impact, such as permaculture principles, renewable energy sources, and organic farming practices.
- Resource efficiency: Focus on optimizing water, energy, and other inputs to reduce waste and lower costs. Techniques such as rainwater harvesting and solar power can significantly contribute to efficiency.
- Economic viability: Ensure that expansion plans are financially sustainable. Budget carefully, explore diverse income streams, and invest in areas with the highest return on investment.

Diversification for Resilience

Diversification is a cornerstone of a resilient homesteading operation. By spreading your efforts across multiple crops, livestock, and income streams, you can buffer against economic and environmental shocks. Benefits of diversification include:

- Risk reduction: Diversifying helps spread risk. If one crop fails or market demand shifts, other aspects of your operation can help sustain overall income.
- Environmental stewardship: Growing various crops and raising different types of livestock can enhance biodiversity, improve soil health, and contribute to a more robust ecosystem on your homestead.
- Adaptability: A diversified operation makes it easier to pivot in response to changing market trends or

environmental conditions. This flexibility is critical to long-term sustainability.

Strategic Planning for Growth

Strategic planning is the blueprint for successful expansion. It involves setting clear objectives, tracking progress, and being willing to adjust plans as circumstances evolve. Essential components of strategic planning include:

- Goal setting: Define what you aim to achieve with expansion, setting specific, measurable, achievable, relevant, and time-bound (SMART) goals.
- Progress monitoring: Establish benchmarks for success and regularly review your progress towards these goals. This might involve tracking financial metrics, production levels, or market penetration.
- Feedback loops: Create mechanisms for receiving feedback, both from within your operation and from customers or clients. This feedback is invaluable for making informed adjustments to your strategy.
- Assessment and adjustment: Be prepared to revise your plans in response to new information, unexpected challenges, or market shifts. Maintaining flexibility allows you to navigate obstacles more effectively and seize new opportunities as they arise.

With these guiding principles, you can ensure that your expansion enhances your homestead and contributes to a legacy of stewardship and resilience.

ADVANCED PERMACULTURE AND LAND MANAGEMENT

Permaculture principles offer a blueprint for living in harmony with our environment. When we scale these principles up, we expand our operations and craft ecosystems that support life in all its diversity. The leap from backyard gardens to expansive, integrated systems requires a deeper dive into permaculture's advanced methodologies.

Permaculture for Large-scale Systems

At its core, permaculture revolves around the symbiotic relationships found in nature. For those managing large swathes of land, the challenge lies in scaling these principles while maintaining their essence. The key is in two design principles:

- Sector planning: By dividing your land into sectors based on natural elements like wind, sunlight, and water flow, you create zones that dictate the most appropriate use for each area, whether for cultivation, livestock, or wildlife habitat.
- Holistic resource management involves seeing your land as a collection of resources that, when managed holistically, enhance the land's overall health and productivity. This might mean rotating livestock to improve soil fertility or planting certain tree species to provide windbreaks and wildlife corridors.

Restorative Land Management Techniques

Restoration plays a crucial role in land management, particularly on homesteads that have inherited land degraded by conventional agricultural practices. Employing restorative techniques heals the land while setting the stage for more resilient and productive homesteading operations. Common restoration strategies include:

- Reforestation: Planting native trees and shrubs prevents soil erosion and restores local wildlife habitat, promoting biodiversity.
- Wetland restoration: Wetlands act as natural water filters and flood buffers. Restoring these areas can improve water quality and provide habitat for aquatic species.
- Soil regeneration: Techniques like biochar application, no-till gardening, and introducing beneficial microbes can revitalize depleted soils, boosting their ability to support diverse plant life.

Water Management Innovations

Efficient water management is crucial for sustainability. Innovative strategies allow for the conservation and optimal use of this precious resource, ensuring that every drop supports the health of your land.

Using a keyline design can be an effective way to manage water across a larger property. This enhances water distribution across the land by aligning cultivation practices with the natural topography to maximize rainwater absorption and reduce runoff.

Constructing artificial wetlands can treat greywater naturally, allowing it to be reused for irrigation. These wetlands also enhance local biodiversity, providing habitat for various species. Additionally, advanced rainwater harvesting systems can capture and store rainwater more efficiently, employing underground cisterns or reservoirs that reduce evaporation and provide a steady water supply during dry periods.

Integrating Technology in Land Management

Fusing traditional land management practices with modern technology enhances efficiency and improves decision-making. By harnessing the capabilities of technological innovations, homesteaders can gain insights into their previously unattainable land. Some options include:

- GIS mapping: Geographic Information System (GIS) technology can map your land in intricate detail, identifying soil types, water sources, and microclimates. This information is invaluable for planning and optimizing land use.
- Drone monitoring: Drones equipped with cameras and sensors can monitor crop health, moisture levels, and pest presence over large areas in real time, providing information that can inform management decisions.
- Remote sensing: Sensors around the homestead can track environmental conditions, from soil moisture to temperature variations, allowing for more precise irrigation and other critical systems management.

By embracing these advanced permaculture and land management strategies, homesteaders can create productive, sustainable, and stimulating systems that breathe new life into the land.

PREPARING FOR EMERGENCIES AND SELF-RELIANCE

Nature is unpredictable, and even the best managed homestead can encounter unexpected emergencies, from sudden storms that threaten crops to power outages that disrupt daily routines. Preparing for the unexpected is wise and vital to ensuring resilience in emergencies.

Foreseeing potential crises requires knowledge about your local environment and understanding your homestead's vulnerabilities. Start with:

- Assessment of risks: Identify the types of natural disasters and emergencies most likely to occur in your area. This awareness forms the bedrock of your planning.
- Evacuation routes and safe zones: Create evacuation routes and designate safe zones within your property. Ensure every family member is familiar with these plans.
- Communication plan: Establish a reliable method for staying in contact with family members in case of separation. Consider alternatives like walkie-talkies in areas with poor cell service.
- Essential documents: Keep important documents, such as identification, property deeds, and insurance papers, in a waterproof, easy-to-carry container.

Building a Homestead Emergency Kit

An emergency kit contains supplies and tools essential for survival during and immediately after a crisis. Tailor your kit to support your household for at least 72 hours, focusing on:

- Water and food: Store at least one gallon of water per person daily and a supply of non-perishable food items. Remember to account for pets and livestock if possible.
- First aid supplies: A well-stocked kit can treat minor injuries and prevent infections. It should also include medications for chronic conditions.
- Power sources: To stay informed, have multiple power sources, such as solar chargers, batteries, and hand-crank radios.

- Tools and protective gear: Include tools necessary for turning off utilities and protective gear like gloves and dust masks.

Self-reliance Skills Training

Beyond physical supplies, the skills you possess are your greatest asset in navigating emergencies. Prioritize learning and practicing:

- First aid and CPR: Knowing how to treat injuries and perform CPR can be life-saving while waiting for medical help.
- Mechanical repairs: Basic knowledge of repairing generators, vehicles, and essential equipment ensures you can address malfunctions quickly.
- Wilderness survival: Skills like building shelters, finding water, and creating fires are invaluable if you are stranded or need to evacuate to remote areas.

Community Emergency Response Networks

In times of crisis, the strength of a community becomes its most powerful resource. Being part of a network that collectively prepares for and responds to emergencies can significantly enhance the resilience of each member. To cultivate such a network:

- Join or form a local group: Connect with or establish a group dedicated to emergency preparedness, which can be within your neighborhood or among the wider homestead community.
- Share resources and knowledge: Organize resource pools for sharing emergency supplies and conduct knowledge exchange sessions on emergency preparedness.

- Coordinate response efforts: Work together to develop plans for evacuation, resource distribution, and emergency aid, ensuring that vulnerable community members receive support.

These actions toward emergency preparedness and self-reliance aren't just items on a checklist; they're fundamental to the homesteading spirit, embodying the principles of stewardship, resilience, and community. By engaging in meticulous planning, diligent preparation, and the cultivation of essential skills, we are prepared to confront any challenges.

LEGACY PLANNING AND PASSING ON SKILLS

The heart of every homesteader beats the desire to cultivate the land and sow the seeds of wisdom for those who will one day walk this path after us. The essence of legacy planning is to ensure the continuity of the homestead's attitudes, knowledge, and resources across generations.

The value of a homestead isn't just about its size or productivity; it's about the legacy it creates. Legacy planning secures the future of the homestead, preserving its values and traditions while offering guidance for future generations, which helps prevent conflicts and facilitates smooth transitions. Such planning honors the hard work and dedication of those who've cared for the homestead, ensuring their legacy continues to grow.

Creating a Succession Plan

A well-crafted succession plan is the cornerstone of effective legacy planning. This plan should encompass:

- Legal considerations: Engage with professionals to address wills, trusts, and legal structures that can protect the homestead and its assets to ensure a smooth transfer of ownership and management.
- Financial planning: Include strategies for managing debt, taxes, and investments to provide financial stability for future generations.
- Operational handover: Document operational procedures, supplier relationships, and customer information. This operational blueprint can be invaluable for those taking over the homestead's day-to-day management.

Teaching and Mentoring

Passing on a legacy relies on transferring knowledge and skills by:

- Hands-on learning: Involve young family members and community members in the daily activities of the homestead.
- Formal education: Encourage formal education in agriculture, sustainability, and business management to complement hands-on learning.
- Mentorship programs: Establish or participate in mentorship programs that pair experienced homesteaders with those eager to learn by fostering a direct line of wisdom and support.

Teaching and mentoring are about transferring knowledge, igniting a passion for the land, and demonstrating a commitment to sustainable stewardship.

Documenting Your Homestead's History and Knowledge

Preserving your homestead's history and accumulated knowledge allows the lessons learned from successes and failures to guide future generations. Methods include:

- Writing a book: Compile your experiences, stories, and advice into a book that can serve as a tangible legacy and inspire others.
- Keeping detailed records: Maintain journals, logs, and records of planting schedules, weather patterns, and financial transactions. These documents provide a wealth of information for analysis and planning.
- Creating digital content: Use blogs, vlogs, and social media to document and share your homestead's journey. This digital footprint can reach beyond your immediate circle, inspiring a broader audience.

Documenting is a powerful tool in legacy planning, transforming individual experiences into collective wisdom that spans generations.

Nurturing our lands and communities, we are inherently involved in legacy building, consciously or unconsciously. Today's steps in planning for the future, teaching the next generation, and preserving our homestead's stories ensure that the fruits of our labor enrich our lives and contribute to the resilience and vitality of the broader homesteading community.

12

INNOVATIONS IN HOMESTEADING:

EMBRACING SMART TECHNOLOGY

In a world where technology touches almost every aspect of our lives, it's no surprise that it has also made its way into homesteading. This chapter illuminates the intelligent technologies that are not just fancy gadgets but tools that can significantly empower a homestead, enhancing its efficiency, productivity, and sustainability.

OVERVIEW OF SMART TECHNOLOGIES FOR HOMESTEADS

Innovative technology in homesteading refers to integrating systems and devices that automate tasks, gather data, and provide insights. These can range from automated irrigation systems that decide when and how much water plants need based on soil moisture levels to energy management systems that optimize power use to livestock monitoring devices that track the health and location of animals.

Imagine a system that can tell you exactly when your tomatoes need watering, like the Smart Irrigation, or a device that alerts you when one of your hens lays an egg, such as the Smart Egg Detector. These aren't scenes from a futuristic movie but real possibilities with today's technology.

The benefits of using innovative technologies on a homestead include:

- Increased efficiency: Automated systems can perform tasks precisely and consistently, reducing waste and optimizing resource use.
- Reduced labor: Automation takes over repetitive tasks, freeing homesteaders to focus on other essential activities requiring human intervention.
- Improved decision-making: Smart devices gather detailed data, offering insights into the best planting schedules and efficient energy use patterns.
- Enhanced animal welfare: Monitoring devices can detect early signs of illness in livestock, allowing for prompt intervention and reducing the risk of widespread health issues.

Considerations and Challenges

While the advantages are compelling, integrating innovative technology into homesteading also comes with its set of considerations:

- Cost: The initial investment for a basic smart technology setup can range from USD 2,000 to 4,000. However, many find that the benefits and savings over time justify the expense.

- Learning curve: Adopting new technology requires time and effort to learn and implement effectively. It's important to note that, like any technology, smart systems are not immune to glitches or malfunctions. Therefore, it's crucial to have a backup plan or manual alternatives in place to ensure the smooth operation of your homestead in case of system failures.
- Balance with traditional practices: It's crucial to balance leveraging technology and maintaining the hands-on, connected approach that defines homesteading.

Future Trends in Smart Homesteading

Technologies currently in their infancy could soon revolutionize how we approach homesteading. For instance, artificial intelligence (AI) assists in analyzing patterns in crop growth and predicting the best times to plant, water, and harvest for maximum yield. Or imagine drones that not only monitor crop health from above but can also perform tasks like planting seeds or dispersing natural pest repellents.

By embracing innovative technologies, homesteaders can make their operations more sustainable and enhance self-sufficiency. When thoughtfully integrated into our age-old practices, these modern tools bridge the gap between tradition and innovation, ensuring our homesteads thrive in the modern era.

NEW DEVELOPMENTS IN RENEWABLE ENERGY

Pursuing renewable energy sources has always been at the heart of the homesteading ethos. Recent years have seen remarkable strides in this arena, with innovations that promise to reshape the landscape of renewable energy. These advancements offer a more sustainable energy solution and contribute to reducing our carbon footprint and mitigating climate change.

Advancements in Solar Energy

Solar energy technology has leaped forward, significantly improving panel efficiency and storage solutions. Modern solar panels now boast higher conversion rates, meaning they can produce more electricity from the same amount of sunlight. This leap in efficiency stems from breakthroughs in photovoltaic cell design and materials, such as using perovskite, a novel material that offers superior light absorption and charge transport properties.

On the storage front, advancements in battery technology, particularly lithium-ion and solid-state batteries, have dramatically enhanced the capacity and lifespan of solar storage systems. These developments allow excess energy generated during sunny periods to be stored more efficiently, ensuring a more consistent and reliable power supply.

Furthermore, solar technology has advanced into innovative applications, such as solar shingles, roofing materials, and transparent solar panels, which can be incorporated into windows. These applications enable more versatile and visually appealing installations, seamlessly integrating solar energy into homestead design.

Emerging Renewable Energy Sources

In addition to solar power, the renewable energy sector has seen the emergence of new sources and technologies that hold potential for homestead applications:

- Wave energy: Harnessing the power of ocean waves represents a promising frontier for renewable energy.

Devices like buoys, turbines, and underwater wings convert the kinetic energy of waves into electricity. For coastal homesteads, wave energy could provide a consistent and abundant power source.

- Biomass energy: The conversion of organic materials into electricity, heat, or fuel through gasification and anaerobic digestion is gaining traction. Homesteaders can leverage biomass energy by converting agricultural waste, such as crop residues and manure, into biogas, a clean and renewable power source.
- New wind turbine designs: More efficient turbine designs, such as vertical-axis turbines, occupy less space and operate effectively at low wind speeds, making them better suited for residential settings.

Integrating Multiple Renewable Sources

Using multiple renewable energy sources maximizes its potential and improves resilience, enhancing energy security by mitigating the variability in renewable sources.

Smart technology can also play a role here. After you set up a hybrid system that combines solar panels, wind turbines, and other renewable sources, you can Utilize smart energy management systems to optimize the use of power based on real-time data and predictive analytics. Implementing grid-tied systems with battery backup allows for exchanging surplus energy with the grid while ensuring autonomy during outages.

Staying Informed on Energy Innovations

The landscape of renewable energy is dynamic, with continuous advancements and breakthroughs. Staying informed about these developments is crucial for homesteaders looking to enhance their energy independence and sustainability. Resources for staying updated include:

- Subscribing to newsletters and journals dedicated to renewable energy and sustainable living.
- Participating in workshops, webinars, and conferences on the latest technologies and practices.
- They engage with online communities and forums where renewable energy enthusiasts share experiences, advice, and insights.

By staying informed about new developments in water purification, homesteaders can take proactive steps toward ensuring the purity of their water. This knowledge empowers them to make informed decisions about adopting and integrating technologies that align with their sustainability goals and water needs.

ADVANCED WATER PURIFICATION TECHNIQUES

There are a variety of groundbreaking water purification technologies tailored for homestead use. Each offers unique advantages, promising to elevate the water purity standard on your property. Some of the most viable options include:

- Solar distillation: This method harnesses the power of the sun to evaporate water, leaving contaminants behind. The vapor then condenses into a separate clean container. Solar distillation units can be constructed with minimal materials, making them a cost-effective solution for homesteaders.
- Biofiltration systems: Biofiltration mimics nature's purification process, using layers of natural materials and beneficial microorganisms to remove impurities from

water. Systems range from simple setups using sand and gravel to more complex constructions incorporating plants known for their purification abilities.
- Advanced rainwater purification: While collecting rainwater is as old as collecting it in agriculture, advancements in filtration and sterilization technology have elevated its purity. Ultrafiltration membranes and UV sterilization lamps can transform rainwater into a potable water source.

Implementing these advanced techniques enhances the quality of water available on your homestead and optimizes its usage. For those incorporating solar distillation, integrating it with irrigation systems reduces the risk of soil contamination and plant diseases.

Biofiltration systems contribute to a closed-loop ecosystem on your homestead by cleaning greywater for reuse in non-potable applications, thereby significantly reducing water wastage. With advanced rainwater purification, the assurance of a clean, reliable water source supports the expansion of homesteading activities without overtaxing local water resources.

DIY Water Purification Projects

For homesteaders keen on self-sufficiency, DIY projects offer a pathway to integrating advanced water purification techniques without expensive commercial systems.

Building a solar distiller can be as straightforward as arranging a black-bottomed basin covered with clear plastic in a sunlit area. This setup allows you to experiment with solar distillation using readily available materials.

Constructing a biofiltration pond might involve digging a small pond and filling it with gravel, sand, and activated charcoal layers.

Planting it with species known for their water-cleaning properties, such as cattails and water hyacinths, adds to its efficiency and aesthetic appeal.

Setting up an advanced rainwater purification system could start with simple first-flush diverters and sediment filters, gradually incorporating more sophisticated elements like UV sterilizers as you scale up.

Assessing Water Purification Needs

A thoughtful assessment of your homestead's water purification needs will ensure you choose the most effective and efficient methods. Considerations include:

- Water source analysis: Testing water from various sources provides a baseline understanding of the contaminants present, such as bacteria, heavy metals, or sediments.
- Usage requirements: Differentiate between water used for irrigation, livestock, and human consumption. Each application has its purity requirements, influencing the choice of purification methods.
- Capacity and scale: Estimate the water needed daily on your homestead to design systems that can handle your demand without excessive overbuilding or wasteful underutilization.

Adeptly managing water champions the health of your homestead embodies the principles of conservation and sustainability, elevates your self-sufficiency, and forges a closer bond with the land.

BIOINTENSIVE GARDENING METHODS

Biointensive gardening is a philosophy that marries the earth's age-old wisdom with the gardener's meticulous care. It aims to cultivate more in less space while nurturing the soil. Rooted in deep soil preparation, dense planting, and the harmonious interplay of plant species, this method transforms the garden into a thriving ecosystem that yields an abundance of crops.

The fundamental principles at the heart of bio-intensive gardening include:

- Deep soil preparation involves loosening the soil up to two feet deep, improving drainage, and allowing plant roots to access more nutrients. This process, often done by hand, enriches the soil structure without disturbing its layers.
- Close plant spacing: By planting crops closer together, gardeners can create a living mulch that retains soil moisture, reduces weed growth, and maximizes yield per square foot.
- Companion planting: This strategy involves placing plants together that benefit one another by repelling pests, attracting beneficial insects, or providing nutrients to each other, creating a symbiotic garden environment.

Benefits of Biointensive Methods

Adopting biointensive gardening methods brings many benefits, not the least of which is a profound connection with the cycle of life. Other advantages include the following:

- Increased yields: Efficiently using space and resources can increase crop yields, providing more food from a smaller area.

- Improved soil health: The emphasis on deep soil preparation and organic amendments enriches soil fertility, encouraging a vibrant, living soil ecosystem.
- More extraordinary biodiversity: Companion planting and using diverse crops support a wider variety of beneficial insects and soil organisms, enhancing garden health.

Implementing Biointensive Practices

Implementing these methods into your garden starts with a detailed plan considering sunlight, soil type, and moisture levels. Select a variety of crops that meet your dietary needs and fit the climate and season. You should choose crops that serve multiple purposes, such as fixing nitrogen or acting as pest deterrents while providing food.

Once you know what you'll plant, invest time deeply aerating your garden beds with a broad fork or garden fork, incorporating well-decomposed compost to nourish the soil. Arrange the plants you've picked in a pattern that optimizes space and encourages symbiotic relationships.

After planting, maintain your garden with regular mulching, careful watering, and hand weeding, continuously monitoring the health of your plants and soil.

Case Studies and Success Stories

To illustrate the transformative power of bio-intensive gardening, consider these real-life examples:

- A small urban homestead in the Pacific Northwest adopted biointensive methods to cultivate its quarter-acre lot. Through deep soil preparation and dense planting, it could

produce 80% of its vegetable needs year-round, significantly reducing its food expenses.
- In a semi-arid region, a homesteader applied biointensive techniques to revive an overworked plot of land. They turned a barren plot into a productive oasis by focusing on soil health and water conservation through close plant spacing and mulching.
- A community garden project utilized companion and dense planting strategies to maximize harvest and engage residents. The success of this project provided fresh produce to the community and served as an educational model for sustainable gardening practices.

These stories underscore the adaptability and effectiveness of biointensive gardening across diverse environments and scales. From small urban plots to larger rural homesteads, these principles offer a path for gardeners to unlock the full potential of their land.

COMMUNITY SUPPORTED AGRICULTURE (CSA) MODELS

Community-supported Agriculture, or CSA, fosters a direct partnership between farmers and consumers. In this model, members buy harvest shares in advance, providing farmers with upfront capital for the growing season. Consumers receive a share of fresh, locally grown produce throughout harvest. This model cultivates a symbiotic relationship, ensuring the sustainability of the homestead while providing the community with nutritious, organically grown food.

Benefits of Starting a CSA

Initiating a CSA program on your homestead secures a market for your produce before the season even begins, alleviating some of the uncertainties of farming. This upfront investment from community members translates into capital that can be used for seeds, equipment, and other necessities, smoothing out financial planning.

Beyond the economic benefits, CSAs strengthen the bond between the homestead and the community. They foster a sense of belonging and mutual support as members get to know their farmer, learn about where their food comes from, and even participate in the farming process through volunteer opportunities.

Challenges and Considerations

While the CSA model is appealing for its community engagement and economic benefits, it also presents particular challenges. Production planning becomes a critical task, as you must accurately predict how much of each crop to plant to meet the needs of all CSA members throughout the season, requiring diligent record-keeping, experience in yield estimation, and sometimes a bit of luck with the weather. Recruiting members presents another challenge, requiring effective marketing strategies and community outreach to ensure enough shares are sold. Additionally, careful consideration is needed for distribution logistics, whether you opt for on-farm pickups, local delivery, or drop-off points.

Innovative CSA Practices

Innovative practices can keep the CSA model vibrant and responsive to the homestead's and its members' needs. Some of these include:

- Educational components: Offering workshops, farm tours, and cooking demonstrations adds value to CSA memberships, engaging members further with the journey of their food from seed to plate.

- Flexible share options: Members can customize their share sizes or choose a "market-style" CSA, where they select their produce each week. This caters to diverse needs and reduces waste.
- Integrating technology: Utilizing websites for member sign-ups, newsletters for farm updates, and social media for sharing the day's harvest connects members digitally to the farm's rhythms, fostering a sense of community outside the farm gates.

The CSA model guarantees a market for the homesteader's produce and engages the community in food production.

The future of homesteading is prosperous and has potential. Through innovation, connection, and a steadfast commitment to sustainability, homesteaders are crafting a vision of agriculture that honors the land and its community.

CONCLUSION

Throughout this book, we have embarked on a transformative journey of off-grid homesteading, which is about survival and thriving. Each step is a testament to your resilience and determination, from the meticulous selection and preparation of your land to the construction of sustainable homes and structures that integrate into the environment rather than impose upon it. We have explored the art of establishing nourishing food sources through gardening and animal husbandry and charted the course toward achieving energy and water independence. Each chapter was a stepping stone in your path toward fostering a robust homestead economy, underpinned by the invaluable support of local farmers, fellow homesteaders, and the broader community.

The critical role of the community cannot be overstated. It is not just a support system but a family that provides resilience and a shared knowledge pool that enriches our journey. In this community, you are not alone. You are part of a collective, a network of individuals who share your passion and are always ready to lend a helping hand.

This is particularly valuable for a venture like an off-grid transition, a journey with challenges and steep learning curves. It demands patience, perseverance, and an open mind willing to absorb new knowledge and adapt to changing circumstances.

As we embark on this sustainable living journey, let us remember it is a continuous learning process. The homesteading landscape is ever-evolving, and true sustainability lies in our adaptability and willingness to embrace continuous improvement. This is not a journey for the faint-hearted but for those willing to learn, grow, and adapt. So, let's stay curious and open to the continuous flow of knowledge, skills, and innovations in sustainable living.

As we strive to live in harmony with our surroundings, let us remember our role as stewards of the environment. We can advocate for sustainable practices within our communities and take proactive steps to reduce our carbon footprint and protect biodiversity. Let's make a conscious effort to be the change we want to see in the world.

I am profoundly grateful for your dedication to exploring off-grid homesteading. Your journey is one of courage and commitment to a life that nourishes the body and the soul. As you move forward, may you find strength in knowing that you are part of a growing community of like-minded individuals, each contributing to a vision of a more sustainable and interconnected world.

In closing, I leave you with a thought from Japanese farmer and philosopher Masanobu Fukuoka:

"The ultimate goal of farming is not the growing of crops, but the cultivation and perfection of human beings."

May your homesteading journey be one of growth, discovery, and fulfillment as you cultivate the land, yourself, and your connection to the earth and one another.

KEEPING THE GAME ALIVE

Now, you have everything you need to start your off-grid homesteading journey, and it's time to pass on your newfound knowledge and show other readers where they can find the same help.

By leaving your honest opinion of this book on Amazon, you'll show other new homesteaders where they can find the information they're looking for and pass on your passion for sustainable living through Off-Grid Homesteading.

Thank you for your help. The spirit of homesteading is kept alive when we pass on our knowledge – and you're helping us to do just that.

Scan the QR code below:

BIBLIOGRAPHY

1. Mother Earth News. (2019, July 5). Consider zoning laws when purchasing homestead land. Mother Earth News. Retrieved June 5, 2024, from https://www.motherearth-news.com/sustainable-living/green-homes/consider-zoning-laws-purchasing-homestead-land-zbcz1907/
2. EOS. (2020, September 10). Soil testing: Types, sampling & interpretation of results. EOS. Retrieved June 5, 2024, from https://eos.com/blog/soil-testing/
3. Homesteading Family. (2020, August 15). Rainwater collection on the homestead. Homesteading Family. Retrieved June 5, 2024, from https://homesteadingfamily.-com/rainwater-collection-on-the-homestead/
4. GreenSwitch Capital. (2020, June 15). How to evaluate your land for solar farm potential. LinkedIn. Retrieved June 5, 2024, from https://www.linkedin.com/pulse/how-evaluate-your-land-solar-farm-potential-greenswitch-capital
5. CNET. (2020, October 20). Living off-grid comes with both savings and hidden expenses. CNET. Retrieved June 5, 2024, from https://www.cnet.com/home/energy-and-utilities/living-off-grid-comes-with-both-savings-and-hidden-expenses/
6. National Sustainable Agriculture Coalition. (2020). Overview: Farm bill programs & grants. Retrieved June 5, 2024, from https://sustainableagriculture.net/publica-tions/grassrootsguide/farm-bill-programs-and-grants/
7. Homesteaders of America. (2020, May 1). 145+ homestead income ideas for the small farm. Retrieved June 5, 2024, from https://homesteadersofamerica.com/income-ideas-small-farm/
8. Salwriter. (2020, November 10). Budgeting for sustainable living: Eco-friendly choices for your wallet and the planet. Medium. Retrieved June 5, 2024, from https://medium.-com/@salwriter/budgeting-for-sustainable-living-eco-

friendly-choices-for-your-wallet-and-the-planet-7ae59d9ca0ae

9. Permaculture Principles. (2020). The 12 permaculture design principles. Retrieved June 5, 2024, from https://permacultureprinciples.com/permaculture-principles/
10. Tiny Shiny Home. (2020, April 5). DIY off-grid solar power system for homestead. Retrieved June 5, 2024, from https://tinyshinyhome.com/diy-off-grid-solar-system
11. U.S. Department of Energy. (2020). Rainwater harvesting systems technology review. Retrieved June 5, 2024, from https://www.energy.gov/femp/rainwater-harvesting-systems-technology-review
12. Direct Compost Solutions. (2020). 8 methods of composting. Retrieved June 5, 2024, from https://direct-compostsolutions.com/8-methods-composting/
13. Elemental Green. (2020). 10 eco building materials revolutionizing home construction. Retrieved June 5, 2024, from https://elemental.green/10-eco-building-materials-revolutionizing-home-construction/
14. Green Building Advisor. (2020, March 20). How to design an off-grid house. Retrieved June 5, 2024, from https://www.greenbuildingadvisor.com/article/how-to-design-an-off-grid-house
15. Agritecture. (2020, October 15). Advancing sustainability through smart greenhouse design. Retrieved June 5, 2024, from https://www.agritecture.-com/blog/2020/10/15/advancing-sustainability-through-smart-greenhouse-design
16. Homesteading. (2020). DIY rainwater collection system for homesteaders. Retrieved June 5, 2024, from https://home-steading.com/diy-rainwater-collection-system/
17. USDA. (2020). USDA plant hardiness zone map. Retrieved June 5, 2024, from https://planthardi-ness.ars.usda.gov/home
18. Eartheasy. (2020). How to make compost using tumblers & bins. Retrieved June 5, 2024, from https://learn.earth-easy.com/guides/composting/
19. Montana State University Extension. (2020). The science of companion planting in the garden. Retrieved June 5,

2024, from https://www.montana.edu/extension/broadwater/blog-article.html?id=18786#:

20. The Old Farmer's Almanac. (2020). How to build a cold frame. Retrieved June 5, 2024, from https://www.almanac.com/how-build-cold-frame
21. Hobby Farms. (2020). Basic farm animal husbandry skills. Retrieved June 5, 2024, from https://www.hobbyfarms.com/basic-farm-animal-husbandry-skills/
22. The Hen House Collection. (2020). Chicken coop ideas for new and existing coops (50+ pictures). Retrieved June 5, 2024, from https://www.thehenhousecollection.com/blog/chicken-coop-ideas-50-pictures/#:
23. Merck Veterinary Manual. (2020). Nutritional requirements of goats: Management and nutrition. Retrieved June 5, 2024, from https://www.merckvetmanual.com/management-and-nutrition/nutrition-goats/nutritional-requirements-of-goats
24. United Nations Environment Programme. (2020). Why bees are essential to people and planet. Retrieved June 5, 2024, from https://www.unep.org/news-and-stories/story/why-bees-are-essential-people-and-planet#:
25. Instructables. (2020). DIY off grid solar system: 12 steps (with pictures). Retrieved June 5, 2024, from https://www.instructables.com/DIY-OFF-GRID-SOLAR-SYSTEM/
26. Kirkwood. (2020). HAWT vs. VAWT – Wind energy. Retrieved June 5, 2024, from https://kirkwood.pressbooks.pub/windenergy/chapter/chapter-3-hawt-vs-vawt/
27. Mother Earth News. (2020). How to make biodiesel: DIY home biodiesel production. Retrieved June 5, 2024, from https://www.motherearthnews.com/sustainable-living/green-transportation/home-biodiesel-production-zm0z15aszmar/
28. Ecotech Daily. (2020). Off-grid battery storage systems: Powering sustainable living. Retrieved June 5, 2024, from https://ecotechdaily.net/off-grid-battery-storage-systems-powering-sustainable-living/
29. WikiHow. (2020). How to build a rainwater collection system. Retrieved June 5, 2024, from https://www.wikihow.com/Build-a-Rainwater-Collection-System

30. Greywater Action. (2020). Greywater reuse. Retrieved June 5, 2024, from https://greywateraction.org/greywater-reuse/
31. WCTNZ. (2020). Composting toilet maintenance 101. Retrieved June 5, 2024, from https://www.wctnz.-co.nz/composting-toilet-maintenance-101
32. Keeper of the Home. (2020). The ultimate guide to homemade all-natural cleaning. Retrieved June 5, 2024, from https://keeperofthehome.org/homemade-all-natural-cleaning-recipes/
33. Barter Exchange of India. (2020). Top 10 benefits of bartering. LinkedIn. Retrieved June 5, 2024, from https://www.linkedin.com/pulse/top-10-benefits-bartering-barter-exchange-of-india-zlqdf#:
34. The Design Trust. (2020). The 39 best places to sell handmade crafts online. Retrieved June 5, 2024, from https://www.thedesigntrust.co.uk/best-places-to-sell-your-crafts-online/
35. Penn State Extension. (2020). Enterprise budgeting for small farms and homesteads. Retrieved June 5, 2024, from https://extension.psu.edu/enterprise-budgeting-for-small-farms-and-homesteads/
36. FindLaw. (2020). 3 things to know before you sell homemade goods. Retrieved June 5, 2024, from https://www.findlaw.com/legalblogs/small-business/3-things-you-to-know-before-you-sell-homemade-goods/
37. Michigan State University Extension. (2020). Benefits of community supported agriculture. Retrieved June 5, 2024, from https://www.canr.m-su.edu/news/principles_and_benefits_of_community_-supported_agriculture
38. University of Minnesota College of Continuing and Professional Studies. (2020). How to start a community garden. Retrieved June 5, 2024, from https://ccaps.um-n.edu/story/7-effective-steps-start-community-garden
39. The Homestead Guide. (2020). 14 online homesteading classes for every budget (free and paid). Retrieved June 5, 2024, from https://thehomesteadguide.com/online-homesteading-classes/

40. Homestead Honey. (2020). 30+ homesteading skills to build with your kids. Retrieved June 5, 2024, from https://homestead-honey.com/30-homesteading-skills-to-build-with-your-kids/
41. Environmental Protection Agency. (2020). Climate change impacts on agriculture and food supply. Retrieved June 5, 2024, from https://www.epa.gov/climateimpacts/climate-change-impacts-agriculture-and-food-supply
42. International Center for Agricultural Research in the Dry Areas. (2020). Drought preparedness and sustainable agriculture. Retrieved June 5, 2024, from https://sustainabledevelopment.un.org/content/documents/2166Drought_preparedness_and_sustainable_agriculture_ICARDA.pdf
43. Asia-Pacific Economic Cooperation. (2017). Guidelines to develop energy resiliency in APEC off-grid areas. Retrieved June 5, 2024, from https://www.apec.org/docs/default-source/publications/2017/5/guidelines-to-develop-energy-resiliency-in-apec-off-grid-areas/toc/main-report.pdf?sfvrsn=a0583559_1
44. Permaculture News. (2020). Implementing a large scale permaculture design in Greece. Retrieved June 5, 2024, from https://www.permaculture-news.org/2020/03/07/implementing-a-large-scale-permaculture-design-in-greece/
45. EOS. (2020). Smart farming: Technologies & benefits for agriculture. Retrieved June 5, 2024, from https://eos.-com/blog/smart-farming/
46. The Guardian. (2023, July 6). 'Revolutionary' solar power cell innovations break key energy threshold. Retrieved June 5, 2024, from https://www.theguardian.com/environment/2023/jul/06/revolutionary-solar-power-cell-innovations-break-key-energy-threshold
47. Sustainable Preparedness. (2020). How to purify water on your off grid homestead. Retrieved June 5, 2024, from https://www.susprep.com/off-grid-water/how-to-purify-water-on-your-homestead/
48. Oakland Institute. (2020). Explore case studies. Retrieved

June 5, 2024, from https://www.oaklandinstitute.org/agroecology-case-studies/explore
49. Contractors. (2020). Do you need a permit for your home project? Retrieved June 5, 2024, from https://www.contractors.com/do-you-need-permit-your-home-project/
50. Agrolearner. (2020). Top 10 free agricultural loan for farmers in USA. Retrieved June 5, 2024, from https://agrolearner.com/agricultural-loan-for-farmers-in-usa/
51. HomeGrid Energy. (2020). Exploring the economics of home energy storage: Solar and battery backup. Retrieved June 5, 2024, from https://www.homegridenergy.com/press/exploring-the-economics-of-home-energy-storage-solar-and-battery-backup
52. Sustainably Forward. (2020). Off-grid sustainable living: 9 important things to know. Retrieved June 5, 2024, from https://sustainablyforward.com/off-grid-sustainable-living/
53. Shapiro. (2020). Top 10 sustainable solutions to reduce food waste. Retrieved June 5, 2024, from https://shapiroe.com/blog/effective-food-waste-solutions/
54. Sustainably Forward. (2020). Small urban permaculture garden: Complete beginners guide. Retrieved June 5, 2024, from https://sustainablyforward.com/small-urban-permaculture-garden/
55. Hearts Content Farmhouse. (2020). How to take care of chickens: Keeping happy hens in your backyard. Retrieved June 5, 2024, from https://heartscontentfarmhouse.com/care-for-chickens-hub/
56. Store Shoppe. (2020). Continuous manufacturing in battery materials: A game-changer. Retrieved June 5, 2024, from https://www.storeshoppe.com/blogs/news/continuous-manufacturing-in-battery-materials-a-game-changer
57. WindCycle. (2020). Small-scale energy revolution: Vertical axis wind turbines for homes. Retrieved June 5, 2024, from https://windcycle.energy/small-scale-energy-revolution-vertical-axis-wind-turbines-for-homes/
58. AIROSD. (2020). Do heat pumps require a lot of maintenance? Retrieved June 5, 2024, from

https://www.airosd.com/article/do-heat-pumps-require-a-lot-of-maintenance.html

59. Diamv. (2020). Power your adventures: Exploring the benefits of DEENO portable power station. Retrieved June 5, 2024, from https://diamv.com/power-your-adventures-exploring-the-benefits-of-deeno-portable-power-station/
60. SolarBlox. (2020). Sustainable home solar battery DIY. Retrieved June 5, 2024, from https://solarblox.co/diy-solar-battery-storage-solutions/
61. Dot Watts. (2020). Solar battery charge time calculator (12v, 24v, 48v). Retrieved June 5, 2024, from https://dotwatts.com/solar-battery-charge-time-calculator/
62. EPElectric LLC. (2020). Home electrical upgrades: A guide to modernize your space. Retrieved June 5, 2024, from https://epelectricllc.com/a-guide-to-modernizing-your-space/
63. Jaymee Srp. (2020). How to passively cool your apartment. Retrieved June 5, 2024, from https://www.jaymeesrp.-com/blogs/all/how-to-passively-cool-your-apartment
64. 13004 Gardening. (2020). What is an irrigation system? Retrieved June 5, 2024, from https://www.13004gardening.com.au/what-is-an-irrigation-system/
65. Suntrics. (2020). How greenhouse farming ensures a steady supply of produce. Retrieved June 5, 2024, from https://suntrics.com/lifestyle-blogs/greenhouse-farming/
66. Call for Content. (2020). How to get your podcast on all platforms. Podcasting Business Guides. Retrieved June 5, 2024, from http://callforcontent.com/how-to-get-your-podcast-on-all-platforms/
67. Stable Income Online. (2020). Ways to make money online with digital marketing. Retrieved June 5, 2024, from https://stableincome.online/online/income/adults/how-to-make-money-online-marketing/
68. Wilmington Real Estate Team. (2020). Boost your business with effective web marketing strategies. Retrieved June 5, 2024, from https://wilmingtonrealestateteam.com/sl-1594847/boost-your-business-with-effective-web-marketing-strategies

69. World Permaculture Association. (2020). 5 ways to protect our waterways. Retrieved June 5, 2024, from https://worldpermacultureassociation.com/5-ways-to-protect-our-water-ways/
70. Masanobu Fukuoka. (n.d.). About Masanobu Fukuoka. Retrieved June 5, 2024, from https://f-masanobu.jp/en/about-masanobu-fukuoka/

OFF-GRID HOMESTEAD COMPANION

Thank you for purchasing Off-Grid Homesteading for Beginners!

As a special bonus, your purchase entitles you to our Off-Grid Homestead Companion, a valuable resource packed with calendars, tools, and tips to help you achieve year-round self-sufficiency.

The download link (QR code) is included below.

We sincerely appreciate your time in reading our book, and we hope this companion enhances your journey. Your feedback is invaluable to us. If you found the book helpful, we would be grateful for an honest review on Amazon. Your feedback helps us grow and reach more like-minded individuals!

www.ingramcontent.com/pod-product-compliance
Ingram Content Group UK Ltd.
Pitfield, Milton Keynes, MK11 3LW, UK
UKHW041637190726
13854UKWH00006B/2552

9 798330 559343